TOPICS IN DISEQUILIBRIUM ECONOMICS

TOPICS IN DISEQUILIBRIUM ECONOMICS

Edited by

Steinar Strøm
University of Oslo

and

Lars Werin
University of Stockholm

These proceedings were originally published in
The Scandinavian Journal of Economics, Vol. 79, 1977, No. 2

First published in book form 1978 by
THE MACMILLAN PRESS LTD
London and Basingstoke
Associated companies in Delhi
Dublin Hong Kong Johannesburg Lagos
Melbourne New York Singapore Tokyo

Printed in Hong Kong

British Library Cataloguing in Publication Data

Topics in disequilibrium economics
1. Equilibrium (Economics)
I. Strøm, Steinar II. Werin, Lars
330′.01′82   HB145

ISBN 0-333-24019-7

CONTENTS

ON QUANTITY SIGNALS AND THE FOUNDATIONS OF EFFECTIVE DEMAND THEORY

Jean-Pascal Benassy*

CEPREMAP, Paris, France

Abstract

This article describes how economic agents rationally formulate their demands when they perceive signals of quantitative disequilibrium. A general definition of effective demand is given for all types of rationing schemes. It is shown to include previously used definitions when rationing is nonmanipulatable, i.e. when each agent faces fixed bounds on his trades. If, on the contrary, he can manipulate these bounds through his demands, rational behavior is shown to lead to an explosive phenomenon of overbidding. Finally the theory is extended to include uncertainty and transaction costs.

I. Introduction

The study of economies out of equilibrium and the integration of micro and macroeconomic theory are subjects which have recently witnessed a considerable renewal of interest. First, following the pathbreaking contributions of Clower (1965) and Leijonhufvud (1968) as well as Bent Hansen (1951) and Patinkin (1965), there have been developments in the theory of effective demand and "Keynesian" equilibria introduced by Barro & Grossman (1971), Benassy (1975a and 1975b), Glustoff (1968) and Grossman (1971). Second, under the impulse of Jacques Drèze (1975), another line of research on non-Walrasian equilibria was developed by Grandmont & Laroque (1976) and Hahn (1975).

Clearly, when confronted with this multiplicity of approaches,[1] one may feel the need for rigorous foundations, as well as a synthetic concept. What we would like to do here is to show that the above approaches can be derived from a decision theory problem, where quantity signals are introduced through a new concept, that of a *perceived rationing scheme*. Indeed we show that both theories derive from the same category, that of perceived non-manipulatable

---

* Thanks to J. M. Grandmont for stimulating me to write this paper.

[1] Indeed a third approach of a game theoretic nature has been proposed by Malinvaud & Younès (1975). As demand and supply functions, which is what we try to derive here, do not appear in their model, we do not consider it in this paper.

rationing schemes, for which the decision problem admits multivalued solutions.

However these are not the only perceived rationing schemes, and we also apply the theory to another category, that of perceived manipulable rationing schemes. Finally it will be extended to include uncertainty or transaction costs.[1]

II. Institutional Setting and Concepts

1. *Markets and Agents*

We consider here, for simplicity, a monetary exchange economy.[2] There are l separate markets on which non-monetary goods ($h = 1, ..., l$) are exchanged against money ($h = 0$). The price of money is 1 and the prices of non-monetary goods are $p_1, ..., p_l$. All these prices will be given below (according to the model, they can be regarded as fixed, or as expected with certainty).[3]

There are n traders in the economy, indexed by i ($i = 1, ..., n$). Trader i acquires on market h a quantity of good h z_{ih} (with the usual sign conventions), giving in exchange a quantity of money $p_h z_{ih}$. The vector of net trades of individual i is thus:

$$z_i = \left(- \sum_{h=1}^{l} p_h z_{ih}, z_{i1}, ..., z_{ih}, ..., z_{il} \right).$$

Individual i has an initial endowment ω_i and a utility function over final transactions $U_i(\omega_i + z_i)$ which we assume strictly quasi-concave. The set of feasible net trades is taken as

$$\{z_i \mid \omega_i + z_i \geqslant 0\}.$$

2. *The Two Institutional Settings*

We consider two different types of institutional arrangements, both of which have been dealt with in the literature:[4]

The first setting, which we will call *tâtonnement*, is somewhat close in spirit

---

[1] An alternative approach to the one of perceived rationing schemes has been developed recently, see Boehm & Levine (1976) and Heller & Starr (1976). It uses essentially a concept of Nash equilibrium with perfect information on the rationing schemes and the actions of other agents.

[2] Non-monetary economies could be considered as well, see Benassy (1976 b); but the notations would become much more complicated.

[3] Schemes for price setting in this type of models can be found in Drèze (1975) for a competitive approach and in Benassy (1976 a), Grandmont & Laroque (1976), Hahn (1975) and Negishi (1974) for a framework of monopolistic competition.

[4] *Tâtonnement* models are found in Barro & Grossman (1971), Benassy (1975 a and 1975 b), Drèze (1975), Glustoff (1968), Grandmont & Laroque (1976), Grossman (1971), and Hahn (1975) and non-*tâtonnement* models in Benassy (1975 a, Appendix) and especially Benassy (1976 b).

to the traditional Walrasian multimarket trading scheme; demands are expressed simultaneously on all markets. Coordination of these demands generally requires some sort of "quantity auctioneer" (hence the name of *tâtonnement*). Trading, consumption (and possibly production) take place only after the "quantity equilibrium" has been reached.

The second setting, which we will call non-*tâtonnement*—not, however, the same kind of non-*tâtonnement* processes as those found e.g. in Hahn & Negishi (1962)—is certainly much closer to what our intuitition of a realistic decentralized monetary economy may be. Each market is organized independently, and individual agents visit these markets one by one, sequentially. No auctioneer is needed to centrally coordinate exchanges; consumption, trading and production can take place dynamically before any equilibrium is reached.

3. *Actions and Consequences*

We begin by giving the main elements of the effective demand approach in terms of decision theory:

Actions of agent i are effective demands expressed on each market h (against money), which we note $\tilde{z}_{ih}$.

Consequences are transactions realized on each market, which we note $\bar{z}_{ih}$. Here we have to distinguish carefully between two concepts:

The *actual consequences* of the actions of the agents are transactions given by the actual trading and rationing rules on each market, which we write:

$$\bar{z}_{ih} = F_{ih}[\tilde{z}_{1h}, ..., \tilde{z}_{nh}].$$

These rationing schemes satisfy the following conditions; see Benassy (1975a):

(α) $\sum\limits_{i=1}^{n} F_{ih}[\tilde{z}_{1h}, ..., \tilde{z}_{nh}] \equiv 0.$

Actual transactions identically sum up to zero

(β) $|\bar{z}_{ih}| \leqslant |\tilde{z}_{ih}| \quad \tilde{z}_{ih} \cdot \bar{z}_{ih} \geqslant 0$

Voluntary exchange

(γ) $\tilde{z}_{ih} \cdot \sum\limits_{i=1}^{n} \tilde{z}_{ih} \leqslant 0 \Rightarrow \bar{z}_{ih} = \tilde{z}_{ih}.$

The agents on the "short" side can realize their demands

(δ) The F_{ih} are continuous.

However, the agent generally does not exactly know the allocation rule or the actions of the other agents. So what will be important in determining his actions is not the actual rationing scheme, but rather the *perceived rationing scheme*, which depicts the way agent i views the relation between his actions and their consequences.

III. The Perceived Rationing Scheme

1. *Observations and Perceived Consequences*

As we said, the agent does not have complete information about the allocation rule or the actions of the other agents. Rather he has made *observations* which constitute his only information. The observations available at the *beginning* of period t to an agent i, and pertaining to a market h, will be denoted $O_{ih}(t)$.

The perceived rationing scheme will give the transaction agent i expects to be able to realize on market h, $\tilde{z}_{ih}^*$, as a function of his action $\tilde{z}_{ih}$, conditionnally on observations available to him $O_{ih}(t)$. This is thus written:

$$\tilde{z}_{ih}^*(t) = \Phi_{ih}[\tilde{z}_{ih} | O_{ih}(t)].$$

We recognize here a concept very similar to the perceived demand curve of monopoly theory; cf. Bushaw & Clower (1957), Negishi (1971) and Benassy (1976a). Note that, by definition, the function Φ_{ih} is of a somewhat subjective nature, contrary to the allocation mechanism F_{ih} which is an objective datum. Typically the observations will include past prices (but we omit them here, as prices are fixed) and quantity signals received in past periods. These signals can be regarded as functions of demands expressed in the past by all the agents. To simplify, we write them as functions of the demands in the preceding periods. This can easily be extended to broader sets of observations; see Benassy (1976c).

$$O_{ih}(t) = G_{ih}[\tilde{z}_{1h}(t-1), ..., \tilde{z}_{nh}(t-1)]$$

A few examples will be presented below. For the moment, we only assume that the G_{ih} (which are usually vector functions) are continuous.

2. *Properties of the Perceived Rationing Scheme*

We now turn to a few general properties which may be expected from the perceived rationing scheme; these properties are evidently related to those of the "objective" transaction mechanism represented by the F_{ih}:

A 1. $\Phi_{ih}[\tilde{z}_{ih} | O_{ih}(t)] \cdot \tilde{z}_{ih} \geqslant 0$
$|\Phi_{ih}[\tilde{z}_{ih} | O_{ih}(t)]| \leqslant |\tilde{z}_{ih}|$.
These two conditions correspond to the idea of voluntary exchange.

A 2. If $\Phi_{ih}[\tilde{z}_{ih} | O_{ih}(t)] = \tilde{z}_{ih}$
then $\Phi_{ih}[\lambda \tilde{z}_{ih} | O_{ih}(t)] = \lambda \tilde{z}_{ih}$ for $0 \leqslant \lambda \leqslant 1$.
This condition expresses the idea that if an agent expects to be unconstrained at some level of demand $\tilde{z}_{ih}$, he should expect to be unconstrained as well for a lower level of demand (in absolute value). This is obviously related to the preceding conditions.

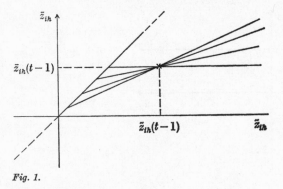

Fig. 1.

A 3. Φ_{ih} is a continuous function of $\bar{z}_{ih}$, $O_{ih}(t)$.

A 4. Finally, we make an assumption of consistency with observations; i.e. *ex post*, observations made should be consistent with the observed consequence regardless of what the effective demands are:

$$\Phi_{ih}[\tilde{z}_{ih}(t-1)\,|\,O_{ih}(t)] \equiv F_{ih}[\tilde{z}_{1h}(t-1),\,...,\,\tilde{z}_{nh}(t-1)].$$

This condition is intuitively very similar to the consistency condition of perceived demand curve theory, see Bushaw & Clower (1957), Negishi (1971) and Benassy (1976 *a*); and can be extended in the same way, see Benassy (1976 *b* and 1976 *c*). Note that this is a property of the triple F_{ih}, G_{ih}, Φ_{ih}. As will be shown in an example below, but can already be seen on a simple graph, this condition is not exceedingly demanding; indeed it only requires the curve $\Phi_{ih}[\tilde{z}_{ih}\,|\,O_{ih}(t)]$ to pass through the point $\{\tilde{z}_{ih}(t-1),\,\bar{z}_{ih}(t-1)\}$ which, as Fig. 1 shows, allows for a wide range of curves.

3. *The Two Types of Perceived Rationing Schemes*

In what follows, it will be useful to distinguish between two types of perceived rationing schemes, which are depicted in Figs. 2 and 3.

(*a*) In the first case (Fig. 2), that of perceived nonmanipulatable rationing schemes,[1] each individual perceives an upper bound ($\bar{\bar{z}}_{ih}^{d}$) and a lower bound ($\bar{\bar{z}}_{ih}^{s}$) on his net trades. The perceived rationing scheme is of the following form:

$$\Phi_{ih}[\tilde{z}_{ih}\,|\,O_{ih}(t)] = \min\,\{\bar{\bar{z}}_{ih}^{d},\,\max\,[\tilde{z}_{ih},\,\bar{\bar{z}}_{ih}^{s}]\}.$$

In this case we adopt the notation

$$\Phi_{ih}[\tilde{z}_{ih}\,|\,O_{ih}(t)] = \Phi_{ih}[\tilde{z}_{ih}\,|\,\bar{\bar{z}}_{ih}(t)] \quad \text{with } \bar{\bar{z}}_{ih} = \{\bar{\bar{z}}_{ih}^{d},\,\bar{\bar{z}}_{ih}^{s}\},$$

since the perceived rationing scheme is entirely determined by the perceived

---

[1] This terminology is found in Grandmont (1976) for the actual rationing schemes.

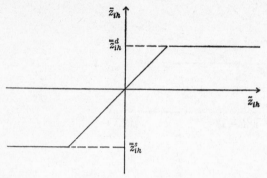

Fig. 2.

constraints $\bar{\bar{z}}_{ih}^{d}$, $\bar{\bar{z}}_{ih}^{s}$. Uniform rationing and queueing (once in the queue) are examples of non-manipulatable rationing schemes.

(b) In the second case (Fig. 3), that of perceived manipulatable rationing schemes, the individual can, even if his transaction is lower than his demand in absolute value, increase the level of his transaction by increasing the level of his demand. However, there is a limit to perceived possible transactions, as no demander can expect to get more than total expected supply (and conversely for a supplier). Proportional rationing is a typical case of a manipulatable rationing scheme.

(c) Note (as we shall see in an example below) that an *actual manipulatable* rationing scheme can give rise to a perceived nonmanipulatable rationing scheme, without violating the conditions above.

4. *An Example*

We now show how a family of perceived rationing schemes can be derived from a given actual rationing scheme when we have some, but incomplete, information.

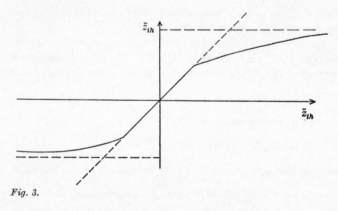

Fig. 3.

Let there be a set I of traders, some demanders (d_i) and some suppliers (s_i). The allocation rule, which we assume known by everybody, is one of proportional rationing, i.e. for example for demander i:

$$d_i = \begin{cases} \tilde{d}_i & \text{if } \sum_{i' \in I} \tilde{d}_{i'} \leqslant \sum_{i' \in I} \tilde{s}_{i'} \\ \tilde{d}_i \cdot \dfrac{\sum\limits_{i' \in I} d_{i'}}{\sum\limits_{i' \in I} \tilde{s}_{i'}} & \text{if } \sum_{i' \in I} \tilde{d}_{i'} \geqslant \sum_{i' \in I} \tilde{s}_{i'} \end{cases}$$

Call $\sum_{i' \in I} \tilde{s}_{i'} = \tilde{s}$ $\sum_{\substack{i' \in I \\ i' \neq i}} \tilde{d}_{i'} = \tilde{d}$.

The rule becomes

$$\tilde{d}_i \begin{cases} \tilde{d}_i & \text{if } \tilde{d}_i + \tilde{d} \leqslant \tilde{s} \\ \tilde{d}_i \cdot \dfrac{\tilde{s}}{\tilde{d}_i + \tilde{d}} & \text{if } \tilde{d}_i + \tilde{d} \geqslant \tilde{s}. \end{cases}$$

Each individual is assumed to receive the same information, which is the rationing proportion:

$$\mu = \frac{\sum_{i' \in I} \tilde{s}_{i'}}{\sum_{i' \in I} \tilde{d}_{i'}} = \frac{\tilde{s}}{\tilde{d}_i + \tilde{d}}.$$

And this is the only *information* he receives, i.e. $O_i(t) = \{\mu(t-1)\}$.

We now assume that individual i believes the others will express the same demands or supplies in the current period as in the previous one. The perceived rationing scheme is thus written (with time indices):

$$\Phi_{ih}[\tilde{d}_i \,|\, O_i(t)] = \begin{cases} \tilde{d}_i & \text{if } \tilde{d}_i + \tilde{d}(t-1) \leqslant \tilde{s}(t-1) \\ \tilde{d}_i \cdot \dfrac{\tilde{s}(t-1)}{\tilde{d}_i + \tilde{d}(t-1)} & \text{if } \tilde{d}_i + \tilde{d}(t-1) \geqslant \tilde{s}(t-1). \end{cases}$$

However, $d(t-1)$ and $s(t-1)$ are both unknown. We only know:

$$\mu(t-1) = \frac{\tilde{s}(t-1)}{\tilde{d}_i(t-1) + \tilde{d}(t-1)}.$$

Let us thus take $\tilde{d}(t-1) = \delta$ as a parameter. $\tilde{s}(t-1) = \mu(t-1)[\delta + \tilde{d}_i(t-1)]$, and the perceived rationing scheme can now be written:

$$\Phi_{ih}[\tilde{d}_i \,|\, \mu(t-1)]$$
$$= \begin{cases} \tilde{d}_i & \text{if } \tilde{d}_i \leqslant \mu(t-1)\,\tilde{d}_i(t-1) + \delta[\mu(t-1) - 1] \\ \tilde{d}_i \cdot \dfrac{\mu(t-1)\,[\delta + \tilde{d}_i(t-1)]}{\delta + \tilde{d}_i} & \text{if } \tilde{d}_i \geqslant \mu(t-1)\,\tilde{d}_i(t-1) + \delta[\mu(t-1) - 1]. \end{cases}$$

It is easy to verify that this function verifies all of the properties we have given, for all values of the parameter δ. In particular it yields:

$$\Phi_{ih}[\tilde{d}_i(t-1)\,|\,\mu(t-1)] = \begin{cases} \tilde{d}_i(t-1) & \text{if } \mu(t-1) \geqslant 1 \\ \mu(t-1)\tilde{d}_i(t-1) & \text{if } \mu(t-1) \leqslant 1 \end{cases}$$

i.e. $\Phi_{ih}[\tilde{d}_i(t-1)\,|\,\mu(t-1)] \equiv \tilde{d}_i(t-1)$ which is consistency condition A4.

Note that for one "true" rationing scheme, even known by everyone, we obtain because of incomplete information a whole family of perceived rationing schemes, indexed by δ. Observe that for $\delta = 0$, we obtain a non-manipulatable perceived rationing scheme.

IV. Generalized effective Demand

Given these preliminaries, derivation of optimal actions for each individual becomes quite straightforward (at least in the simple model without uncertainty or transaction costs we have been considering so far). They will be the ones which maximize the utility of consequences (i.e. transactions) given the perceived relation between effective demands and transactions. We now give two expressions, corresponding to the *tâtonnement* and non-*tâtonnement* versions, respectively.

1. *Tâtonnement*

Here, all effective demands $\tilde{z}_{ih} h = 1, ..., l$ are determined simultaneously on the l markets and will thus be given by the following program:

$$\begin{cases} \text{Maximize } U_i(\omega_i + \tilde{z}_i) \\ p\tilde{z}_i \leqslant 0 \\ \omega_i + \tilde{z}_i \geqslant 0 \\ \tilde{z}_{ih} = \Phi_{ih}[\tilde{z}_{ih}\,|\,O_{ih}(t)] \quad \forall h = 1, ..., l. \end{cases}$$

2. *Non-tâtonnement*

In this case markets are visited sequentially (in an order which we assume identical to the natural order $1, .., l$) and effective demands are expressed one by one on each market. So when agent i arrives on market h, he has already carried transactions $\bar{z}_{ik}(t)$ on markets visited before $h(k < h)$, so that his program is:

$$\begin{cases} \text{Max } U_i(\omega_i + \tilde{z}_i) \\ p\tilde{z}_i \leqslant 0 \\ \omega_i + \tilde{z}_i \geqslant 0 \\ \tilde{z}_{ik} = \bar{z}_{ik}(t) & 1 \leqslant k < h \\ \tilde{z}_{ik} = \Phi_{ik}[\tilde{z}_{ik}\,|\,O_{ik}(t)] & k \geqslant h.[1] \end{cases}$$

---

[1] We omit liquidity-type constraints, as they will vary widely according to the model considered; cf. Clower (1967).

Note that here only $\tilde{z}_{ih}$ actually has to be determined by this program. The $\tilde{z}_{ik}$, $k > h$ are conditional plans not announced by the agent.

3. *A Two-Step Procedure*

As we shall see, it may be fruitful to determine demands by first finding the optimal expected transaction and then the associated demand. We explain the procedure in the *tâtonnement* case. Let us first define the set of attainable transactions

$$\bar{Z}_i[O_i(t)] = \{z_i \mid \forall h \exists \tilde{z}_{ih} \quad \text{s.t.} \quad z_{ih} = \Phi_{ih}[\tilde{z}_{ih} \mid O_{ih}(t)]\}.$$

Now the set of feasible transactions, denoted $\gamma_i[p, O_i(t)]$, is the set defined by:

$$\begin{cases} pz_i \leqslant 0 \\ \omega_i + z_i \geqslant 0 \\ z_i \in \bar{Z}_i[O_i(t)]. \end{cases}$$

The optimal expected transaction $\tilde{z}_i$ will be the solution of

Maximize $U_i(z_i)$ on $\gamma_i[p, O_i(t)]$,

and the set of demands will simply be determined by:

$$\tilde{z}_{ih} = \Phi_{ih}^{-1}[\tilde{z}_{ih} \mid O_i(t)],$$

where $\Phi_{ih}^{-1}[\cdot \mid O_i(t)]$ is evidently the inverse correspondence of $\Phi_{ih}[\cdot \mid O_i(t)]$.

V. Perceived Non-manipulatable Rationing Schemes in *Tâtonnement* Models: A Problem of Definition

We now come to the problem which we hinted at in the introduction, i.e. how can the two existing definitions of demands be reconciled? As we shall see, both definitions pertain to the category of perceived nonmanipulatable rationing schemes. For this case the generalized effective demand is a multivalued application, if which the two above demands are the most interesting special cases. We begin by giving the relevant definitions.

1. *Definitions; the Two Demands*

As we said above, the perceived rationing scheme will have the following particular form:

$$\tilde{z}_{ih} = \Phi_{ih}[\tilde{z}_{ih} \mid \bar{z}_{ih}] = \min\{\bar{z}_{ih}^d, \max\{\tilde{z}_{ih}, \bar{z}_{ih}^s\}\}.$$

This will imply that expected transactions belong to the interval of perceived constraints, i.e.:

$$\bar{z}_{ih}^s \leqslant \tilde{z}_{ih} \leqslant \bar{z}_{ih}^d.$$

(a) The Drèze constrained demands are determined simultaneously on all markets.

The vector of demands is given by the following program:

Maxizime $U_i(z_i)$ over $\gamma_i[p, \bar{\bar{z}}_i]$

where $\gamma_i[p, \bar{\bar{z}}_i]$ is the following set:

$$\begin{cases} pz_i \leqslant 0 \\ \omega_i + z_i \geqslant 0 \\ \bar{\bar{z}}_{ih}^s \leqslant z_{ih} \leqslant \bar{\bar{z}}_{ih}^d \quad \forall h \neq 0. \end{cases}$$

(We can note that this is the set of expected transactions.) The vector of constrained demands will be denoted $\hat{z}_i[p, \bar{\bar{z}}_i]$.

(b) The Clower-type effective demands—actually found, in the form given here, in e.g. Benassy (1975a)—are determined separately on each market. Effective demand on market h, $\tilde{z}_{ih}$, is the hth component of the solution of the following program:

Maximize $U_i(z_i)$ over $\gamma_{ih}[p, \bar{\bar{z}}_i]$

where $\gamma_{ih}[p, \bar{\bar{z}}_i]$ is the following set:

$$\begin{cases} pz_i \leqslant 0 \\ \omega_i + z_i \geqslant 0 \\ \bar{\bar{z}}_{ik}^s \leqslant z_{ik} \leqslant \bar{\bar{z}}_{ik}^d \quad \forall k \neq 0, h. \end{cases}$$

Effective demand on market h is denoted $\tilde{z}_{ih}[p, \bar{\bar{z}}_i]$, and the vector of effective demands $\tilde{z}_i[p, \bar{\bar{z}}_i]$ (a vector of dimension l, since there are l markets).

2. The Problem Posed

The existence of at least two definitions suggests (unless one of them is inconsistent, but it will be shown this is not the case) that our generalized effective demand definition might admit multivalued solutions. Intuitively, this will indeed happen—even with strictly quasiconcave utility functions—for constrained individuals, because in this case the correspondence Φ_{ih}^{-1} is actually multivalued. This can be seen most clearly in the Edgeworth box example in Fig. 4.

The economy has two individuals and a single market. The price is not the equilibrium one, and OA, OB are the tangency points of the indifference curves of agents 1 and 2, respectively.

Assume first that each agent knows exactly the quantitative constraint he faces (as is the case in *tâtonnement* models). Then clearly agent 1's generalized effective demand is OA. Agent 2's demand, however, can according to our definition be anywhere between OA and OC. Among all these possibilities,

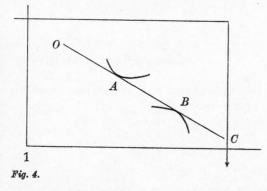

Fig. 4.

Drèze's demand corresponds to OA and Clower's corresponds to OB. Both will yield the same level of expected transaction (but the latter presents the advantage of giving some measure of disequilibrium).

3. *Formal Statements*

We now make the above heuristic arguments more formal. We show that effective demands of the Drèze and Clower type belong to the set of generalized effective demands.

Call $\tilde{Z}_i[p, \bar{z}_i]$ the generalized effective demand.

Proposition 1. *Drèze's demand belongs to the generalized effective demand:*

$$\hat{z}_i[p, \bar{z}_i] \in \tilde{Z}_i[p, \bar{z}_i].$$

This is a totally trivial property since $\hat{z}_i$ maximizes $U_i(z_i)$ over $\gamma_i[p, \bar{z}_i]$, and by construction:

$$\Phi_{ih}[\hat{z}_{ih} | \bar{z}_{ih}] = \hat{z}_{ih}.$$

We can indeed note that Drèze's theory is such that actions are always identical to their expected consequences, so that in the program giving optimal demands the perceived constraints act as direct constraints on the actions.

Proposition 2. *Clower-type effective demand belongs to the generalized effective demand*

$$\tilde{z}_i[p, \bar{z}_i] \in \tilde{Z}_i[p, \bar{z}_i].$$

This amounts to showing that if $\tilde{z}_{ih} = \Phi_{ih}[\tilde{z}_{ih} | \bar{z}_{ih}]$, then $\tilde{z}_i$ maximizes $U_i(z_i)$ over $\gamma_i[p, \bar{z}_i]$, i.e. showing that $\tilde{z}_i = \hat{z}_i$.

(α) Assume first $\tilde{z}_{ih} \in [\bar{z}_{ih}^s, \bar{z}_{ih}^d]$.

12   *J.-P. Benassy*

Then:

$$\bar{z}_{ih} = \Phi_{ih}[\tilde{z}_{ih} \,|\, \bar{\bar{z}}_{ih}] = \tilde{z}_{ih}.$$

The maximum of U_i over γ_i and γ_{ih} is the same, which implies that $\tilde{z}_{ih} = \hat{z}_{ih}$. The two together yield $\bar{z}_{ih} = \hat{z}_{ih}$.

(β) Assume now $\tilde{z}_{ih} \notin [\bar{\bar{z}}_{ih}^s, \bar{\bar{z}}_{ih}^d]$, for example $\tilde{z}_{ih} > \bar{\bar{z}}_{ih}^d$ (the argument would be exactly symmetrical for $\tilde{z}_{ih} < \bar{\bar{z}}_{ih}^s$).

Then:

$$\bar{z}_{ih} = \Phi_{ih}[\tilde{z}_{ih} \,|\, \bar{\bar{z}}_{ih}] = \bar{\bar{z}}_{ih}^d$$

$\tilde{z}_{ih}$ maximizes U_i over γ_{ih}

A simple convexity argument shows that we must have: $\hat{z}_{ih} = \bar{\bar{z}}_{ih}^d$. The two together again yield $\bar{z}_{ih} = \hat{z}_{ih}$.

We will now prove a property which somewhat justifies effective demand as the exchange actually demanded on the market, or as the best measure of disequilibrium (though the justification will be valid essentially for non-*tâtonnement* models).

Proposition 3. *Clower-type effective demand on a market belongs to the generalized effective demand for all possible constraints on that market:*

$$\tilde{z}_{ih}[p, \bar{z}_i] \in \tilde{Z}_{ih}[p, \bar{z}_i] \quad \forall \bar{\bar{z}}_{ih}.$$

Note that this is a strong property because $\tilde{z}_{ih}$ does not depend on $\bar{\bar{z}}_{ih}$. It can be also translated as the following property:

$\tilde{z}_{ih}$ maximizes U_i over $\gamma_{ih}(p, \bar{z}_i)$

$\hat{z}_i$ maximizes U_i over $\gamma_i(p, \bar{z}_i)$.

Then, for any $\bar{\bar{z}}_{ih}$, $\Phi_{ih}[\tilde{z}_{ih} \,|\, \bar{\bar{z}}_{ih}] = \hat{z}_{ih}$.

Take a particular $\bar{\bar{z}}_{ih}$. Then the reasoning used to prove proposition 2 is valid, and

$$\Phi_{ih}[\tilde{z}_{ih} \,|\, \bar{\bar{z}}_{ih}] = \hat{z}_{ih}.$$

But this reasoning is clearly valid for any $\bar{\bar{z}}_{ih}$, which demonstrates the proposition.

VI. Perceived Nonmanipulable Rationing Schemes in Non-*Tâtonnement* Models

A property such as property 3 above could be used to eliminate the indeterminacy in the generalized effective demand. However, it is clearly not an "operational" property in the *tâtonnement* setting for two reasons: (a) it pertains to one market at a time, while demands are announced on all markets together in the *tâtonnement* setting, and (b) more importantly, the agent will never have to announce a demand without ignoring the "true" constraint, since transactions are not carried out before a quantity equilibrium is reached.

But these very two reasons will make *a contrario* the analogue of Proposition 3 highly relevant in the case of the non-*tâtonnement* setting. Indeed in the corresponding models, demands are expressed on one market at a time, and moreover they have to be expressed before the constraint is known. The "true" constraint $\bar{z}_{ih}$ will be revealed to the agent during the transaction process, that is after demands have been emitted, so that even if the agent has point expectations, these will generally turn out to be wrong. In this context a proposition similar to Proposition 3 would mean that effective demand of the Clower type is the dominant strategy.

Returning to our simple example in Fig. 4 may help our intuition. If agent 2 has to announce his demand before knowing the constraint OA he will face, there is one, and only one, demand which will be the solution of the optimization program whatever the constraint OA; this is OB, the effective demand of the Clower type, which is the only admissible strategy. We can now proceed to a more formalized statement, and proof, after a few definitions.

Generalized effective demand on market h, $\tilde{Z}_{ih}$, is given by the following program (seen above in its general form):

Maximize $U_i(\omega_i + \tilde{z}_i)$

$$\begin{cases} p\tilde{z}_i \leqslant 0 \\ \omega_i + \tilde{z}_i \geqslant 0 \\ \tilde{z}_{ik} = z_{ik}(t) & k < h \\ \tilde{z}_{ik} = \Phi_{ik}[\tilde{z}_{ik} \,|\, \bar{\tilde{z}}_{ik}(t)] & k \geqslant h. \end{cases}$$

Effective demand of the Clower type, $\tilde{z}_{ih}$, is given by (see Benassy, 1975a, Appendix):

Maximize $U_i(\omega_i + z_i)$

$$\begin{cases} pz_i \leqslant 0 \\ \omega_i + z_i \geqslant 0 \\ z_{ik} = z_{ik}(t) & k < h \\ \bar{\tilde{z}}_{ik}^s(t) \leqslant \tilde{z}_{ik} \leqslant \bar{\tilde{z}}_{ik}^d(t) & k > h. \end{cases}$$

Note that in both cases we are only interested in the hth component of the optimal vectors (as the other components for $k > h$ are only expectations not communicated to the market).

We can now state the following:

Proposition 4

$\tilde{z}_{ih} \in \tilde{Z}_{ih} \quad \forall \bar{\tilde{z}}_{ih}.$

One just needs to notice that the set of possible expected transactions is the following set:

$$
\begin{cases}
pz_i \leqslant 0 \\
\omega_i + z_i \geqslant 0 \\
z_{ik} = \bar{z}_{ik}(t) & k < h \\
\bar{z}_{ik}^s \leqslant z_{ik} \leqslant \bar{z}_{ik}^d(t) & k \geqslant h.
\end{cases}
$$

and apply exactly the same technique as in Propositions 2 and 3.

Proposition 4 allows us to ascertain that in a dynamic model, Clower-type effective demand will be the one actually transmitted to the market, as it is the only admissible action for the agent (taking here the constraint on market h $\bar{z}_{ih}$ as the "unknown state of the world").

VII. Manipulatable Rationing Schemes: A Problem of Dynamics and Equilibrium

1. *The Problem*

We now come to the category of perceived manipulatable rationing schemes and thus revert to the general notation for the perceived rationing scheme:

$$
\Phi_{ih}[\tilde{z}_{ih} \,|\, O_{ih}(t)].
$$

As the problem is very similar in the *tâtonnement* and the non-*tâtonnement* settings, we do not consider them separately.

In this case problems do not arise from the definition itself. Indeed we can apply the procedure indicated in the definition of generalized effective demand. First determine the desired consequence on market h, $\bar{z}_{ih}(t)$, by maximizing utility over the set of expected possible consequences, then derive generalized effective demand by:

$$
\tilde{z}_{ih}(t) = \Phi_{ih}^{-1}[\bar{z}_{ih}(t) \,|\, O_{ih}(t)]
$$

which is single-valued in this case.

However, what will happen intuitively is that each constrained individual (i.e. for which $\bar{z}_{ih}$ is different from $\tilde{z}_{ih}$) will "overbid", i.e. express a demand quite higher than the transaction he expects to obtain. But if there are many constrained individuals who act the same way, this process will lead to a displacement of the perceived transaction curve as shown in Fig. 5, which means that in order to attain the same level of transactions, traders will have to express continuously increasing demands.

In terms of our models, this means that effective demands would either be determined by more or less artificial boundary conditions (which is quite uninteresting economically) or go to infinity (i.e. there would be no equilibrium).

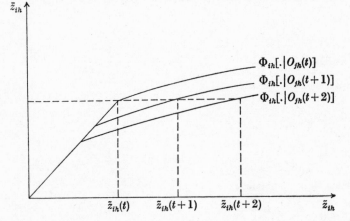

Fig. 5.

2. *An Example*

The following very simple example can be used to illustrate the above problem. Consider an economy with a single market with proportional rationing, one supplier ($\tilde{s}$) and two demanders ($\tilde{d}_1, \tilde{d}_2$). The rationing rule is thus:

$$\tilde{d}_1(t) \begin{cases} \tilde{d}_1(t) & \text{if } \tilde{d}_1(t) + \tilde{d}_2(t) \leqslant \tilde{s}(t) \\[2ex] \tilde{d}_1(t) \cdot \dfrac{\tilde{s}(t)}{\tilde{d}_1(t) + \tilde{d}_2(t)} & \text{if } \tilde{d}_1(t) + \tilde{d}_2(t) \geqslant \tilde{s}(t). \end{cases}$$

Assume each trader knows the rationing rule and the demands of the others after they have been expressed, and expects these demands to remain the same in the following period. The perceived rationing scheme for trader 1 is thus:

$$\Phi_1[\tilde{d}_1 \mid O_1(t)] = \begin{cases} \tilde{d}_1 & \text{if } \tilde{d}_1 + \tilde{d}_2(t-1) \leqslant \tilde{s}(t-1) \\[2ex] \tilde{d}_1 \cdot \dfrac{\tilde{s}(t-1)}{\tilde{d}_1 + \tilde{d}_2(t-1)} & \text{if } \tilde{d}_1 + \tilde{d}_2(t-1) \geqslant \tilde{s}(t-1). \end{cases}$$

Each trader has a "target transaction level" (resulting from unconstrained utility maximization) which he wants to achieve in each period, and which we denote $\hat{d}_1, \hat{d}_2, \hat{s}$.

We assume:

$\hat{d}_1 + \hat{d}_2 > \hat{s}$ so that we have the case where two individuals on the same side of the market are constrained.

$\hat{d}_1 < \hat{s}, \hat{d}_2 < \hat{s}$ so that each of the demanders perceives he can achieve his target transaction level.

Given these assumptions, effective demands in each period t will be given by:

$$\tilde{s}(t) = \hat{s} \quad \forall t$$

$$\Phi_1[\tilde{d}_1(t) \,|\, O_1(t)] = \hat{d}_1$$

$$\Phi_2[\tilde{d}_2(t) \,|\, O_2(t)] = \hat{d}_2.$$

The last two equations yield:

$$\tilde{d}_1(t) = \tilde{d}_2(t-1) \cdot \frac{\hat{d}_1}{\hat{s} - \hat{d}_1}$$

$$\tilde{d}_2(t) = \tilde{d}_1(t-1) \cdot \frac{\hat{d}_2}{\hat{s} - \hat{d}_2}.$$

Combining them we obtain:

$$\tilde{d}_1(t) = \tilde{d}_1(t-2) \cdot \frac{\hat{d}_1}{\hat{s} - \hat{d}_1} \frac{\hat{d}_2}{\hat{s} - \hat{d}_2},$$

which forms a divergent sequence, given our assumption that $\hat{d}_1 + \hat{d}_2 > \hat{s}$.

VIII. Extensions to Uncertainty and Transaction Costs

We now show briefly how the concepts of a perceived rationing scheme and generalized effective demand can be extended to the case where uncertainty or transaction costs are present.

1. *Uncertainty, the General Case*

Instead of being a function, perceived rationing will rather have the form of a joint probability distribution over demands $\tilde{z}_{ih}$ (the actions) and transactions $\bar{z}_{ih}$ (the consequences), and this probability distribution will depend on the information available $O_i(t)$

$$\Psi'_i[\tilde{z}_i, \bar{z}_i \,|\, O_i(t)].$$

Generalized effective demand will be obtained by maximizing the expected utility of final transactions with respect to that probability distribution, subject to all budget and positivity constraints.

We can remark that the presence of uncertainty might to some extent stop the phenomenon of overbidding in the manipulable case, if the individuals were actually obliged to keep their final transactions for their personal use, since by overbidding too much they could end up with unwanted quantities of goods. However, there is usually some ex-post reallocation in such markets (through black-market, resale at the same price, bartering for other goods, etc.), which makes it safe, and even profitable, to end up with too many rationed goods, so that in these cases overbidding is likely to prevail, even in the presence of uncertainty.

2. *Uncertainty, the Nonmanipulatable Case*

In this case the perceived rationing scheme simplifies somewhat as it will become:

$$\tilde{z}_{ih} = \min \{\bar{\bar{z}}_{ih}^d, \max \{\tilde{z}_{ih}, \bar{\bar{z}}_{ih}^s\}\} = \Phi_{ih}[\tilde{z}_{ih}|\bar{\bar{z}}].$$

But this time perceived constraints $\bar{\bar{z}}_{ih}$, instead of being expected with certainty, are given by a joint probability distribution:

$$\Psi_i[\bar{\bar{z}}_i|O_i(t)].$$

Temporary equilibria using such distributions have been studied in Benassy (1975*a*) in the *tâtonnement* setting.[1] For the non-*tâtonnement* setting, the following stochastic analogue to Proposition 4 has been proved by Futia (1975) in the case of two markets (with, in addition, a number of counterexamples) and extends readily to:

Proposition 5. *Consider a sequence of markets in a non-tâtonnement setting where the perceived constraints are independently distributed, i.e.:*

$$\Psi_i[\bar{\bar{z}}_i|O_i(t)] = \Psi_{i1}[\bar{\bar{z}}_{i1}|O_{i1}(t)] \times ..$$
$$\times \Psi_{ih}[\bar{\bar{z}}_{ih}|O_{ih}(t)] \times ... \times \Psi_{il}[\bar{\bar{z}}_{il}|O_{il}(t)].$$

Then $\tilde{z}_{ih}$, the effective demand on market h, does not depend upon Ψ_{ih}.

Proof. Consider a sequence of transactions $z_{i1} ... z_{ih}$ and the sum of money m_{ih} held at the end of this sequence

$$m_{ih} = \omega_{i0} - \sum_{k=1}^{h} p_k z_{ik},$$

and associate to these an "indirect utility function"

$$V_{ih}[m_{ih}, z_{i1}, ..., z_{ih}]$$

which is the expected utility of this sequence of transactions provided optimal actions are taken in the future. This indirect utility function does not depend on $\bar{\bar{z}}_{i1} ... \bar{\bar{z}}_{ih}$ because of the independence assumption seen above. Obviously the indirect utility function for the last market is the original utility function, i.e.:

$$V_{il}[m_{il}; z_{i1}, ..., z_{il}] \equiv U_i(\omega_{i0} + z_{i0}, ..., \omega_{il} + z_{il})$$

with $m_{il} = \omega_{i0} - \sum_{k=1}^{l} p_k z_{ik} \equiv \omega_{i0} + z_{i0}.$

---

[1] Note that in a *tâtonnement*, uncertainty has to be restricted to future periods, since current transactions are "auctioneer-coordinated".

The functions V_{ih} are determined recursively by the following relation:

$$V_{ih-1}[m_{ih-1}, z_{i1}, ..., z_{ih-1}]$$
$$= \text{Max} \int V_{ih}[m_{ih-1} - p_h \Phi_{ih}[\tilde{z}_{ih} | \bar{\bar{z}}_{ih}], z_{i1}, ..., z_{ih-1}, \Phi_{ih}(\tilde{z}_{ih} | \bar{\bar{z}}_{ih})] d\Psi_{ih}(\bar{\bar{z}}_{ih}),$$

which also determines $\tilde{z}_{ih}$. Concavity of V_{ih}[1] implies that the unconstrained maximum of $V_{ih}[m_{ih-1} - p_h z_{ih}, z_{i1}, ..., z_{ih}]$ with respect to z_{ih} will yield the solution $\tilde{z}_{ih}$, which is independent of $\Psi_{ih}(\bar{\bar{z}}_{ih})$. Note that $\tilde{z}_{ih}$ is as well the maximum of $V_{ih}[m_{ih}, z_{i1}, ..., z_{ih-1}, z_{ih}]$ subject to $p_h z_{ih} + m_{ih} = m_{ih-1}$.

3. Transaction Costs

In general, transaction costs may be associated either with expressing demands, or with realizing transactions, which we write:

$$c_i = \chi_i[\tilde{z}_i, \bar{z}_i].$$

These costs will appear along with final transactions in the utility function, which we write:

$$U_i(\omega_i + \bar{z}_i - c_i).$$

The program giving the generalized effective demand will become (shown here for the *tâtonnement* case, which simplifies notations):

$$\begin{cases} \text{Max } U_i(\omega_i + \bar{z}_i - c_i) \\ \tilde{z}_i = \Phi_i[\tilde{z}_i | O_i(t)] \\ c_i = \chi_i[\tilde{z}_i \cdot \bar{z}_i] \\ p\bar{z}_i = 0 \\ \omega_i + \bar{z}_i - c_i \geqslant 0. \end{cases}$$

It can be remarked that in reality, while costs associated with transactions vary monotonously, those associated with demands will rather be of the fixed costs type (they are simply the costs of going to the market or participating in it). As a result, in the non-manipulatable case the multivaluedness problem will remain. However, we may also have a property such as Proposition 4, as illustrated by the following simple example.

An example. Assume a single market for some good. The cost (in money) of expressing a demand is:

$$c(\tilde{d}) = \begin{cases} 0 & \text{if} \quad \tilde{d} = 0 \\ c & \text{if} \quad \tilde{d} > 0. \end{cases}$$

The price is p. Initial endowment of the trader is $(m_0, 0)$. His utility function is $U(m, \tilde{d})$, where m is his final holding of money,

$$m = m_0 - p\tilde{d} - c(\tilde{d}).$$

---

[1] Proof of the concavity of V_{ih} is easy but tedious and is thus omitted here. It uses basically the same techniques as in Benassy (1975a, Section 7).

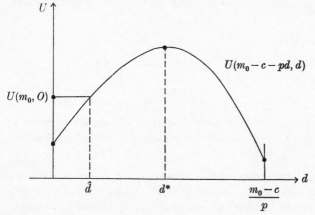

Fig. 6.

The program which gives the generalized effective demand will simply be:

Max $U(m_0 - p\tilde{d} - c(\tilde{d}), d)$

$\tilde{d} = \min(\hat{d}, \bar{\bar{d}})$,

where $\bar{\bar{d}}$ is the expected constraint on the market.

Now call d^* the unconstrained maximum of $U(m_0 - pd - c, d)$ and $\hat{d}$ the solution of:

$$U(m_0 - pd - c, d) = U(m_0, O).$$

Assume also that $d^* > \hat{d}$ (if not, there could be no trading on the market anyway). It is then easy to see, with the help of Fig. 6, that:

For $\hat{d} < \bar{\bar{d}} < d^*$, the generalized effective demand is multivalued.
However, d^* belongs to the generalized effective demand for all $\bar{\bar{d}} > \hat{d}$, which
is a property similar to Proposition 4.

4. *Manipulation through transaction costs*

Throughout this paper we have assumed that the level of transactions was influenced solely by the agents' demands. However, a most important aspect of rationing procedures in reality is that they can also be manipulated through some sort of transaction costs. Accordingly, the perceived rationing scheme will be written:

$$\tilde{z}_i = \Phi_i[\tilde{z}_i, c_i \,|\, O_i(t)],$$

i.e. transaction will depend on demand and the cost the agent will have chosen to bear in order to manipulate the outcome. In this case the program which yields generalized effective demand (along with optimal transaction costs) would be:

Max $U_i(\omega_i + \bar{z}_i - c_i)$ s.t.

$$\begin{cases} p\bar{z}_i = 0 \\ \omega_i + \bar{z}_i - c_i \geqslant 0 \\ \bar{z}_i = \Phi_i[\tilde{z}_i, c_i \,|\, O_i(t)]. \end{cases}$$

It actually appears that most rationing schemes encountered in reality are non-manipulatable through demand, but manipulatable through some costs. We give two simple examples:

In all systems such as queues, priority systems, etc. it is clear that an agent cannot manipulate through demand once his ranking is known. However, this ranking can be modified at a cost, such as arriving earlier in a queue.

In oligopolistic markets, the maximum sales that each firm will make will not be influenced by its supply, but rather by price variations and especially marketing expenses.

In such cases, the formalization becomes:

$$\bar{z}_i = \min\{\bar{z}_i^d, \max(\tilde{z}_i, \bar{z}_s^i)\}$$

with $\bar{z}_i = \mu_i[c_i \,|\, O_i(t)]$,

where c_i is again the "manipulation cost". The fact that the costs enter the objective function negatively prevents demands and costs in this case from diverging, as we observed in the case of manipulation through demand.

IX. Conclusion

In this paper a new tool of analysis, the perceived rationing scheme, was developed which gives the expected relation between the demand and the transaction of an agent on a market in disequilibrium (this concept thus has a status, with respect to the true rationing scheme, similar to the concept of a perceived demand curve with respect to the "true" demand curve in monopoly theory). This analytical tool could be extended to include uncertainty as well as transaction costs. It allowed us to construct, quite naturally, a decision program yielding the optimal demands in disequilibrium, which we called generalized effective demand. The structure of the problem led to a distinction between two polar cases.

In the first case, perceived non-manipulatable rationing schemes, each agent perceives "non-manipulatable" bounds on his level of transactions. This has been the case studied in the literature up to now; the two definitions of demand mainly studied (associated with the names of Clower and Drèze) were both shown to belong to generalized effective demand, which in this case admits multivalued solutions (at least in the absence of uncertainty).

The second case, perceived manipulatable rationing schemes, where rationed agents can positively influence the level of their transactions by increasing their demands, was shown to induce a phenomenon of "overbidding". This made demands expressed a very unreliable measure of disequilibrium, and moreover led to an explosive dynamic behavior of demands, so as to make equilibrium inexistent or meaningless.

Perceived non-manipulatable rationing schemes thus appear the most suitable for the construction of macroeconomics-oriented models. In this case, however, there remains the problem of choosing the most suitable expression of demand. The above arguments seem to indicate that demand of the Clower type is a natural tool when a measure of disequilibrium on a market is required, when price setting agents are introduced, or when a dynamic model is to be constructed, especially if uncertainty is present. However, further research is certainly needed as more general stock-flow models are developed.

References

Barro, R. J. & Grossman, H. I.: A general disequilibrium model of income and employment, *American Economic Review*, March 1971.

Benassy, J. P.: Neokeynesian disequilibrium theory in a monetary economy. *Review of Economic Studies*, October 1975*a*.

Benassy, J. P.: Disequilibrium exchange in Barter and monetary economies. *Economic Inquiry*, June 1975*b*.

Benassy, J. P.: The disequilibrium approach to monopolistic price setting and general monopolistic equilibrum. *Review of Economic Studies*, February 1976*a*.

Benassy, J. P.: Regulation of the wage-profits conflict and the unemployment-inflation dilemna in a dynamic disequilibrium model. *Economie Appliquée*, no. 3, 1976*b*.

Benassy, J. P.: Théorie du déséquilibre et fondements microéconomiques de la macroéconomie. *Revue Economique*, September 1976*c*.

Boehm, V. & Levine, J. P.: Temporary equilibria with quantity rationing. Core Discussion Paper, 1976.

Bushaw, D. W. & Clower, R. W.: *Introduc-*

tion to mathematical economics, Richard D. Irwin, Homewood, Ill. 1957.

Clower, R. W.: The Keynesian counter-revolution: A theoretical appraisal. In F. H. Hahn & F. P. R. Brechling (Eds.), *The theory of interests rates*, Proceedings of an I. E. A. Conference. Macmillan, London, 1965.

Clower, R. W.: A reconsideration of the micro-foundations of monetary theory. *Western Economic Journal*, December 1967.

Drèze, J.: Existence of an equilibrium under price rigidity and quantity rationing. *International Economic Review*, 1975.

Futia, C.: A theory of effective demand. Mimeo, Bell Laboratories, May 1975.

Glustoff, E.: On the existence of a Keynesian equilibrium. *Review of Economic Studies*, 1968.

Grandmont, J. M.: Temporary general equilibrium theory. CEPREMAP Discussion Paper, January 1976, to appear in *Econometrica*.

Grandmont, J. M. & Laroque, G.: On temporary Keynesian equilibria. *Review of Economic Studies*, February 1976.

Grossman, H. I.: Money, interest and prices in market disquilibrium. *Journal of Political Economy*, September 1971.

Hahn, F. H.: On non-Walrasian equilibria. Mimeo, Stanford, 1975.

Hahn, F. H. & Negishi, T.: A theorem on non-tatonnement stability. *Econometrica* 1962.

Heller, W. P. & Starr, R. M.: Unemployment equilibrium with rational expectations. IMSSS Working Paper, Stanford University, 1976.

Hansen, B.: *A study in the theory of inflation.* Allen and Unwin, London, 1951.

Leijonhufvud, A.: *On Keynesian economics and the economics of Keynes.* Oxford University Press, London, 1968.

Leijonhufvud, A.: Effective demand failures. *The Swedish Journal of Economics,* March 1973.

Malinvaud, E & Younes, Y.: Une nouvelle formulation générale pour l'étude des fondements microéconomiques de la macroéconomie. INSEE and CEPREMAP, Paris, 1975.

Negishi, T.: Monopolistic competition and general equilibrium, *Review of Economic Studies,* June 1971.

Negishi, T.: Involuntary unemployment and market imperfection. *Economic Studies Quarterly,* April 1974.

Pattinkin, D.: *Money, interest and prices,* 2nd ed. Harper and Row, New York, 1965.

THE LOGIC OF THE FIX-PRICE METHOD

Jean-Michel Grandmont

CEPREMAP, Paris, France

Abstract

Recent works on the microeconomic foundations of macroeconomics (Barro & Grossman, Benassy, Malinvaud, Younès) make use of the Hicksian fix-price method. In these studies, prices are assumed to be temporarily fixed in the short run, and adjustments take place through quantity rationing. A basic assumption of these models is that only agents on the "long side" of a market are rationed (e.g. buyers when there is an excess demand). This paper surveys some recent contributions to the study of the logic of this assumption. It is argued in particular that, although these models are designed to describe "disequilibrium" states where there is an excess demand or supply on some markets, their logic appears to involve some kind of recontracting process at fixed prices among traders.

I. Introduction

Following the impulse of Clower (1965) and Leijonhufvud (1968), recent works on the microeconomic foundations of macroeconomics have focused attention on models of the non-*tâtonnement* type where exchange can take place at non-Walrasian prices; cf. Hahn & Negishi (1962). In these models, quantitative constraints on trade, as perceived by the agents, play a central role in the analysis, in addition to the price system.

A good deal of the progress made in this area has been achieved by the study of a simple and extreme case, where prices are temporarily fixed in each period. The structure of these models is as follows. At the outset of any given period, prices are quoted, e.g. by the sellers, in the light of their past experience and their expectations of the state of the economy in the coming and future periods. Once these prices are quoted, they cannot be changed until the next period. At these prices, the demands and supplies currently expressed *ex ante* by the agents may not be compatible. In that case, it is postulated that there is an allocation mechanism (or a rationing scheme) which makes the agents' realized (or *ex post*) transactions sum to zero. Then the economy moves to the next date and new prices may be quoted. The rules obeyed by an allocation mechanism in these studies are simple. If at the ruling prices, the demand and supply currently expressed by the agents on a given market are compatible, then all agents should realize their plans. If there is an excess demand, then all sellers should realize their plans, while some buyers must be rationed, i.e. compelled to buy less than they intended.

These models turn out to be useful tools for analyzing some issues which traditionally belong to the realm of macroeconomic theory. In particular, it is possible to reach a temporary equilibrium where there is an excess supply both in the market for the output of firms and in the labor market, that is, which displays Keynesian unemployment. But these models can generate other situations as well, for instance, one in which there is an excess demand for output and an excess supply of labor (stagflation or classical unemployment), or one in which there is an excess demand in both markets (repressed inflation); see the series of contributions by Barro & Grossman, and the work of Benassy (1973 and 1974), Hildenbrand (1976), Malinvaud (1976), Negishi (1974) and Younès (1970b).

In order to motivate the analysis in this paper, I sketch briefly a simple analytical example which has been extensively studied by Barro & Grossman, Benassy, Malinvaud and Younès. The specification I use is that of Benassy (1974) and the reader will find detailed computations in his work.

There are two aggregated economic agents, households and firms, and three goods, output, labor and money (denoted Y, L and M). The prevailing money price and wage are p and w. There are two markets on which output and labor are exchanged against money at ruling prices.

Firms produce output with labor according to the production function $Y = F(L)$, which is concave, increasing, twice differentiable and such that $F'(0) = +\infty$. Firms do not invest nor do they hold inventories. Profits $\pi = pY - wL$ are distributed to the households.

On the other hand, households have a utility function $U(Y, M/P, L_0 - L)$, where $L_0 - L$ is leisure, which can be viewed as an indirect utility function derived from an intertemporal utility maximization problem, as is usual in temporary equilibrium models. Following Benassy, I take the specific form

$$U = \alpha_1 \log Y + \alpha_2 \log (M/P) + \alpha_3 \log (L_0 - L).$$

The households' budget constraint is

$$pY + wL + M = M_0 + \pi$$

where π is the firms' profit and M_0 is the initial money endowment.

Under these assumptions, there is a unique Walrasian equilibrium p^*, w^*. When p and/or w differ from these values, equilibrium is reached by means of quantitative constraints perceived by the agents. It turns out that there are three types of equilibria which can be obtained:[1]

1. *Keynesian unemployment*, where there is an excess supply in both markets. Households cannot sell all the labor they want, and firms' production is constrained by the households' effective demand.

2. *Classical unemployment*, where there is an excess supply of labor and an

---

[1] The terminology I use is that of Malinvaud (1976).

excess demand for output. Households are constrained on both markets, while firms are unconstrained.

3. *Repressed inflation*, where there is an excess demand in both markets. Firms cannot hire as much labor as they want at prevailing prices and wages, and households cannot buy as much output as they would like.

The fourth possibility, where the firms are constrained in both markets and the households are unconstrained reduces in this model to a degenerate case at the limit between Keynesian unemployment and repressed inflation. This is due to the fact that firms cannot be constrained in both markets unless one of the constraints is redundant (this case would reappear if firms were allowed to invest or to hold inventories).

It turns out that under the above assumptions, there is a unique equilibrium associated with given values of p, w and M_0. It belongs to one, and only one, of the types mentioned. Moreover, if p, w and M_0 are multiplied by the same positive number, all real quantities describing the associated equilibrium are unchanged. It is therefore possible to represent the different regimes that can be obtained in a $(w/p, M_0/p)$ diagram, which can be partitioned into three regions (see Fig. 1). When $(w/p, M_0/p)$ belongs to region I, described by OWA, the associated equilibrium displays Keynesian unemployment. Output and employment are given by

$$Y = \frac{\alpha_1}{\alpha_2} \frac{M_0}{p}, \quad L = F^{-1}(Y).$$

Region II corresponds to classical unemployment. Output and employment are given by the firms' profit maximizing problem and depend only on the real wage w/p. Region III corresponds to repressed inflation. Employment and output are given by

$$L = L_0 - \frac{\alpha_3}{\alpha_2} \frac{M_0}{w}, \quad Y = F(L).$$

It follows that lines of equal output and employment are represented by triangles such as $a\ b\ c$ in Fig. 1, and that output grows as one moves towards inner triangles and towards the Walrasian equilibrium W.

A few interesting (but by no means exhaustive) remarks can be made about this diagram.

A decrease in the nominal wage (p and M_0 being fixed) has very different consequences on the level of employment, depending on the prevailing regime. In the case of classical unemployment, it increases employment, as was claimed by the classics. On the other hand, it has no effect on output in the case of Keynesian unemploymnt.

An increase in initial cash balances (p and w being fixed) increases output in the case of Keynesian unemployment, but has no effect in the case of classical unemployment.

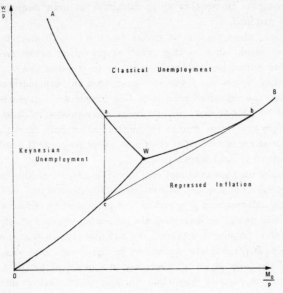

Fig. 1

The conclusions reached through this example should not be taken too seriously, of course, at this stage. A great deal of research is needed before general and accepted conculsions can be obtained. In particular, it would be desirable to have models with a more apparent intertemporal structure, where the role of expectations which is so central in Keynesian thinking is made precise, and where monetary and fiscal policy have a meaningful role to play. The example shows, however, that the equilibrium concept used is an interesting one, because it enables us to discuss, within a unified framework, macroeconomic theories which were previously regarded as fundamentally distinct.

I purposely used the word "equilibrium" in this discussion, rather than the term "disequilibrium" which is often employed in this field. This essay will clarify the reasons for this. But it may be useful to discuss this point informally at this stage. It is true that in the models under scrutiny, the final allocation in a given period may involve an excess demand or supply in some market, that is, there may be a "disequilibrium" in some market, in contrast to the classical Walrasian model, where all markets clear. Prices may therefore display some tendency to move from period to period in response to such "disequilibria". In any given period, however, the final allocation in these models is the result of a *tâtonnement* on quantities. One reason is that there is a simultaneous adjustment on several markets. Indeed since the constraints perceived by an agent on a given market will influence his effective demand or supply on another market, the final allocation on some market may depend strongly on the existence and extent of disequilibria on others (spillover effects). Another reason is embodied in a fundamental assumption made in these models, that is the fact that the agents on the "short side" of the market always realize their plans (e.g. the sellers if there is an excess demand). In an economy with many buyers and sellers, this postulate appears to imply some *tâtonnement* among traders, so that eventually at the *ex post* allocation, no seller is left with an unsold good when there is an excess demand. Indeed it will be shown later on that some kind of recontracting appears to be involved in this notion of equilibrium.

The first studies of this concept of equilibrium in a general equilibrium framework seem to have been made by Younès (1970*a*, 1970*b* and 1975), by Drèze in a paper which circulated in 1971 and was published in 1975, and by Benassy (1973, 1974 and 1975). In Section II below I discuss two basic models which are currently used in the field, Drèze (1975) and Benassy (1975). In Section III, I study the efficiency properties of such equilibria. I then show, by using the theory of games in Section 3, that contrary to the usual views this concept of equilibrium appears to involve some notion of "recontracting" (at fixed prices).

II. Market Equilibrium with Quantity Rationing[1]

Consider an economy in a given period. There are $l+1$ commodities to be exchanged, indicated by $h=0, 1, ..., l$, good 0 being money. Prices are quoted at the outset of the period, and they are described by a vector p in the interior of the unit simplex Δ^{l+1} of R^{l+1} which will remain fixed throughout the analysis. There are m agents indicated by $a=1, ..., m$. The ath agent's set of feasible net trades is denoted Z^a, a subset of R^{l+1}. The ath agent's actual transactions z must belong to Z^a and satisfy the budget constraint $p \cdot z = 0$.

In addition to the quoted price system, for each commodity h other than money, a trader perceives quantitative constraints $\underline{z}_h^a$ and $\bar{z}_h^a$ that set lower and upper bounds to the amount of commodity h that he can trade. An important assumption of the model is that no constraint is perceived in the case of commodity 0. One reason for this assumption is to avoid trivial equilibria involving no trade, as we shall see below. A particular *interpretation* of the model is that there are l separate trading posts, one for each commodity h other than money, where the traders exchange commodity h against money at ruling prices. Although these markets are separated, the traders are supposed to trade simultaneously in all of them. Indeed, for every $h \neq 0$, let $t(h)$ be the elementary transaction describing an exchange of one unit of commodity h gainst $-(p_h/p_0)$ units of money: $t(h)$ is a vector in R^{l+1} which satisfies

---

[1] The material in this section is based on Grandmont (1975, Section 3.1).

$t_0(h) = -(p_h/p_0)$, $t_h(h) = 1$ and $t_k(h) = 0$ for $k \neq 0, h$. Then every trade such that $p \cdot z = 0$ can be written $z = \sum_{h=1}^{l} z_h t(h)$, and conversely.

In this interpretation, z_h can be viewed as the intensity of the transaction of commodity h for money, and the constraints $\underline{z}_h^a$ and $\bar{z}_h^a$ can be interpreted as constraints on these intensities. Commodity 0 then plays the role of a medium of exchange in the same way as demand deposits, and it can be imagined that payments at each trading post are made by writing out checks or by making use of a credit card, the only requirement being that a trader's final money balances must satisfy some *a priori* given constraints embodied in the definition of the feasible set Z^a.

The ath agent's preferences among commodities are described by a complete preordering $\succsim_a$ defined on Z^a. These preferences can be derived by a standard dynamic programming technique as is susual in temporary equilibrium models. In general, they depend on the signals received by the agent up to the date under consideration (in particular, on current prices and perceived quantitative signals) through their influence on the agent's expectations. In order to focus our attention on the essentials, however, I assume that the preordering $\succsim_a$ is independent of current signals. This restriction can easily be relaxed.

I begin with Drèze's model (1975). Let $s^a = (\underline{z}^a, \bar{z}^a)$ be the signal perceived by the ath trader, where $\underline{z}^a$ and $\bar{z}^a$ are vectors in R^l and satisfy $\underline{z}^a \leqslant \bar{z}^a$. Given this signal, each trader expresses his constrained excess demand, represented by a subset $\zeta(s^a)$ of Z^a.

This will be the result of the maximization of the agent's preferences on the set $\gamma^a = \{z \in Z^a \,|\, p \cdot z = 0 \text{ and } \underline{z}_h^a \leqslant z_h \leqslant \bar{z}_h^a, \ h \neq 0\}$.

A *Drèze equilibrium* is described by a set of signals $s = (s^a)$ and by net trades $z^a \in \zeta^a(s^a)$ such that

(α) $\sum_{a=1}^{m} z^a = 0$.

(β) for each $h \neq 0$, $z_h^a = \bar{z}_h^a$ for some a implies $z_h^b > \underline{z}_h^b$ for all b;
    and $z_h^a = \underline{z}_h^a$ for some a implies $z_h^b < \bar{z}_h^b$ for all b.

(γ) $\underline{z}^a \leqslant 0 \leqslant \bar{z}^a$, for all a.

Condition (β) means that only traders on one side of the market for commodity h may perceive binding constraints, which is quite natural. Condition (γ) is a "voluntary exchange" condition, saying that no trader can be forced to exchange more than he wishes. These two conditions imply that agents on the short side of the market (the sellers if buyers perceive binding contraints) always realize their plans.

Lemma 1 (Drèze, 1975). *Assume*

(i) Z^a *is closed, convex, bounded below and* $0 \in Z^a$;

(ii) $\succsim_a$ *is continuous and convex.*

Then, there exists a Drèze equilibrium.

I omit the proof of this result, which makes use of a standard fixed point argument.

The structure of the model makes clear the type of adjustment which takes place implicitly in this economy. There is some "auctioneer" who quotes quantitative constraints z^a and $\bar{z}^a$. In response to these constraints, sets of constrained excess demands $\zeta^a(s^a)$ are sent to the market by the traders. If the auctioneer registers, say, an excess demand for some commodity $h \neq 0$, he lowers the upper bounds $\bar{z}_h^a$ imposed upon the traders' purchases. Any fixed point of this *tâtonnement* in quantity constraints is an equilibrium in the Drèze sense.

The foregoing definition of an equilibrium does not specify how shortages are distributed among agents. Consequently, there will be many equilibria (in general, a continuum). In order to develop a more specific theory, it is natural to require that the final outcome of the trading process correspond to a given rationing scheme. It is indeed possible to modify the above definition of an equilibrium, and the proof of Lemma 1, so as to take some specific rationing schemes into account.[1] For instance, a *uniform* rationing requires that all constraints z^a and $\bar{z}^a$ do not depend on the trader (Drèze, 1975). It is equally straightforward to take care of the case where rationing on a market h must occur according to some given order (*queuing*). The case where the rationing scheme depends on trade offers made by the agents which might violate the constraints $z_h^a \leqslant z_h \leqslant \bar{z}_h^a$, $h \neq 0$, as in the case of proportional rationing, falls outside the scope of Drèze's model, since such trade offers are not considered (a precise formulation of such rationing mechanisms will be given below when I study Benassy's model). It would be interesting to see how Drèze's model should be amended in order to handle such general rationing schemes. It is important to see that the central problem in this approach is the formulation of a satisfactory theory explaining why, in the light of the quantitative constraints z^a and $\bar{z}^a$ which they perceive, the agents would express trade offers differing from those in $\zeta^a(s^a)$.

An alternative and interesting attempt to model an equilibrium with quantity rationing has been implemented by Benassy (1973 and 1975). His model is a generalization of the work of Barro & Grossman (1971) and of Grossman (1971). Instead of assuming, as Drèze did, that the traders send their constrained demands to the market, he postulates that they send trade offers which may violate the constraints they perceive. By a rationing mechanism these trade offers, in turn, determine the agents' actual transactions. From these, the traders formulate new offers. An equilibrium is defined by Benassy as a fixed point of this process in the space of trade offers.

More precisely, assume that the ath agent sends to the market a trade offer $\tilde{z}^a \in R^l$, representing his excess demand for each commodity $h \neq 0$. No trade

---

[1] See Grandmont (1975).

offer is made for money; this corresponds to the idea which I have already mentioned that money is used as a medium of exchange or at least acts as a buffer stock. Let $\tilde{z} \in R^{lm}$ be the vector of all trade offers made by the agents. These offers may not be compatible, that is $\sum_{a=1}^{m} \tilde{z}^a$ may differ from zero. Benassy postulates that there is a rationing scheme which associates to $\tilde{z}$ an *ex post* transaction $z_h^a = F_h^a(\tilde{z})$ for each trader and each commodity $h \neq 0$. This rationing scheme is supposed to satisfy the following natural conditions for every $\tilde{z} \in R^{lm}$ and every $h \neq 0$:

(a) $\sum_{a=1}^{m} F_h^a(\tilde{z}) = 0$;

(b) $z_h^a \tilde{z}_h^a \geqslant 0$ and $|z_h^a| \leqslant |\tilde{z}_h^a|$, which means that the sign of an agent's transaction cannot be reversed, and that no one can be forced to exchange more than he wishes;

(c) the agents on the "short" side of the market realize their plan, that is, $\tilde{z}_h^a(\sum_{a=1}^{m} \tilde{z}_h^a) \leqslant 0$ implies $z_h^a = \tilde{z}_h^a$. These conditions are closely related to (β) and (γ) in the definition of a Drèze equilibrium.

The *ex post* transactions z_h^a, $h \neq 0$, determine the agent's *ex post* transaction z_0^a in money by $p_0 z_0^a = -\sum_{h=1}^{l} p_h z_h^a$. This gives an *ex post* trade $z^a \in R^{l+1}$ which satisfies $p \cdot z^a = 0$ and is a function of $\tilde{z}$ alone. I might remark that there is no guarantee that z^a is feasible, that is, we may have $z^a \notin Z^a$. I shall come back to this point later on.

The comparison of his original offer with his *ex post* transactions makes a trader perceive subjective quantity constraints $\underline{z}^a \in R^l$ and $\bar{z}^a \in R^l$ on his trades of commodities $h \neq 0$, as in Drèze's model. The perception of these constraints may also be influenced by whatever information the trader has about the other agents' trade offers. As all of this information is a function of $\tilde{z}$ alone, I write $\underline{z}^a = \underline{G}^a(\tilde{z}) \leqslant 0$ and $\bar{z}^a = \bar{G}^a(\tilde{z}) \geqslant 0$. The functions $\underline{G}^a$ and $\bar{G}^a$ are given data of the problem and are assumed to satisfy for every $h \neq 0$ and $\tilde{z} \in R^{lm}$:

(d) $\underline{G}_h^a(\tilde{z}) \leqslant z_h^a \leqslant \bar{G}_h^a(\tilde{z})$;

(e) $\tilde{z}_h^a > z_h^a$ implies $\bar{G}_h^a(\tilde{z}) = z_h^a$, and $z_h^a > \tilde{z}_h^a$ implies $\underline{G}_h^a = z_h^a$.

In the case where $\tilde{z}_h^a > z_h^a$, for instance, z_h^a must be nonnegative from condition *b*. It is then natural to assume that the trader perceives he cannot buy more than z_h^a of commodity h. Other conditions where imposed by Benassy but they will not be needed in the sequel.

I now turn to the crucial assumption of Benassy's model which pertains to the determination of the agents' trade offers. Following Barro & Grossman (1971) and Grossman (1971), he assumes that a trader's demand on some market $h \neq 0$ is the result of the maximization of his preferences ignoring the constraints associated with this commodity, but taking into account the constraints perceived on the other markets. More precisely, for every $h \neq 0$, consider the hth component of the net trades which maximize $\succsim_a$ in the set $\gamma_h^a = \{z \in Z^a \,|\, p \cdot z = 0 \text{ and } \underline{z}_k^a \leqslant z_k \leqslant \bar{z}_k^a, \, k \neq 0, h\}$. They form a subset of the real line

$\zeta_h^a(\tilde{z})$. The operation is repeated for every $h \neq 0$, and the ath agent's set of trade offers $\zeta^a(\tilde{z})$, a subset of R^l, is taken as the product of all $\zeta_h^a(\tilde{z})$. The product of all $\zeta^a(\tilde{z})$, $a = 1, ..., m$, is denoted $\zeta(\tilde{z})$. Then Benassy defines an equilibrium as a point $\tilde{z}$ in R^{lm} such that $\tilde{z} \in \zeta(\tilde{z})$.

Lemma 2 (Benassy, 1975). *Assume*

(i) *Z^a is closed, convex, bounded below and $0 \in Z^a$;*

(ii) *the functions F_h^a, $\underline{G}^a$ and $\bar{G}^a$ are continuous;*

(iii) *the preordering $\succsim_a$ is continuous and convex.*

Then, there exists a Benassy equilibrium.

The proof of this result, which I omit, makes use of a straightforward fixed point argument.

Apart from the mere question of existence, an equilibrium must satisfy other conditions. Any equilibrium $\tilde{z}$ determines perceived constraints $\underline{z}^a$ and $\bar{z}^a$, and an *ex post* trade z^a which satisfies $p \cdot z^a = 0$. A natural requirement is that z^a be feasible, $z^a \in Z^a$ and, furthermore, that z^a maximizes the trader's preferences in the set $\gamma^a = \{z \in Z^a \,|\, p \cdot z = 0, \ \underline{z}_h^a \leqslant z_h \leqslant \bar{z}_h^a, \ h \neq 0\}$. There is nothing in the proposed definition which guarantees these properties. This is due to the fact that the agents' trade offers are formulated in the model independently on each market h, and without taking their consequences (final trades) into account. If these two requirements, especially the first, were not met, it is quite likely that the agents would revise the way they formulate their trade offers. Checking whether these two conditions are satisfied in equilibrium therefore provides a test of the logical consistency of the model. It turns out that they are satisfied when the preferences $\succsim_a$ are strictly convex, but that they may not be otherwise.

Lemma 3 (Benassy). *Under the assumptions of Lemma 2, at a Benassy equilibrium $\tilde{z}$, the final transactions z^a belong to Z^a and maximize the preferences $\succsim_a$ on the set γ^a, provided that $\succsim_a$ is strictly convex for each a.*

I omit the proof of this result, which is not difficult. The following example shows that when the preferences $\succsim_a$ are not strictly convex, z^a may not belong to Z^a. Assume that there are three commodities ($l = 2$), two traders a and b and that all prices are equal. Suppose that agent a's feasible set is $Z^a = \{z \,|\, z + w^a \geqslant 0\}$ where the endowment of money w_0^a is such that $1 \leqslant w_0^a < 2$, and that his set of most preferred trades in the set of $z \in Z^a$ such that $p \cdot z = 0$ contains the closed segment joining the two trades $(-1, 1, 0)$ and $(-1, 0, 1)$. Assume that the other trader's most preferred trade happens to consist of selling one unit of each commodity 1 and 2. A possible "equilibrium" in the Benassy sense would be a situation where trader a offers to buy one unit of each commodity 1 and 2, but he cannot afford it. This shows that some

Benassy equilibria may not be sensible when the preferences $\succsim_a$ are not strictly convex. However, it seems that under the assumptions of Lemma 2, there always exists a Benassy equilibrium such that $z^a \in Z^a$ and z^a maximizes $\succsim_a$ on γ^a (approximate each $\succsim_a$ by a sequence of preorderings which are strictly convex, apply Lemma 2 for each element of the sequence, and go to the limit).

The most interesting feature of Benassy's model is the fact that it can handle general rationing schemes, which Drèze's model cannot do, at least in its present state. The weak point of course, is how the agents formulate their trade offers, which does not seem to be justified by a satisfactory theory. These trade offers are made independently on each market, without considering their consequences on final transactions. I have already pointed out that this might lead to inconsistencies in some cases. At any rate, since the trade offers $\tilde{z}^a$ are in general altogether infeasible for a trader, caution should be taken when using them as a measure of the size of disequilibrium, as is often done in some studies of the dynamics of such models. All this points to the need for a better theory explaining how traders formulate trade offers in the presence of constraints on their transactions, a fact that I mentioned earlier in connection with Drèze's model. One possible line of attack is to assume that the agents know the rationing scheme, and that, given the trade offers of the other agents, each trader sends trade offers on all markets so as to maximize the utility of their consequences. This leads to a concept of Nash equilibrium in the space of trade offers; on these points see Benassy (1976), Boehm & Levine (1976) and Heller & Starr (1976).

Drèze's model may be criticized on the grounds that it does not generate an exchange of information among traders about the size of the rationing that they experience. On the other hand, in Benassy's model, the trade offers $\tilde{z}^a$ do not appear to be reliable measures of the size of disequilibrium in each market, for the reasons I have already mentioned. Accordingly, it may be argued, the agents who control some prices do not know whether and by how much to change them in the next trading period. This issue seems essential to any dynamic study of the model, where price changes come into play. But the picture is not as bad as it appears, for the models can be amended and applied to situations where such information does exist. The concept of equilibrium, as it stands, tells us who the agents are who are constrained in commodity h. It can be assumed that this information is at least partly available to the other traders, in which case they know that there is a disequilibrium on some market and have information on the number of agents who perceive binding constraints. But more importantly, the traders do have information about the size of the disequilibrium in this model if they know the final trades of the other agents and if we interpret some markets as future markets (to be precise, the theory presented in this section would have to be extended, since the Z^a can no longer be assumed bounded below in the presence of future markets). Indeed, in many cases, a buyer who is prevented from purchasing a commodity in the current period will place an order to obtain the same commodity at some specified or unspecified later date. To the extent that he makes a downpayment, this can be interpreted as a forward contract of a special type (or a couple of forward contracts; a purchase of the commodity by the buyer with full payment of the price in the current period, and a loan from the seller to the buyer). In such a case, sellers can have some information about the size of the excess demand for some commodity by looking at the size of purchases on the corresponding future market. Other relevant indicators are the level of stocks in the case of durable goods, and of leftovers otherwise. In the special case of the labor market, where future markets typically do not exist, it is safe to assume that a specific agent, the government, pays unemployment benefits which, again, generates information about the size of unemployment. In the light of all this information, the traders would forecast supplies or demands for the future periods, and would make up their minds about possible revisions of the prices they control for the next trading period. This seems to be a realistic way of modelling the flows of information which actually take place in our economies. A difficult but rewarding project would be to study a model along these lines and to look at its dynamic implications.

The Drèze and Benassy concepts of equilibrium have the following characteristics in common. First, for each commodity $h \neq 0$, only one side of the market is constrained. And second, no trader can be forced to exchange more than he wishes. These two principles imply that the agents on the "short" side of the market always realize their plans. These remarks lead me to adopt the following definition of equilibrium, for the remainder of this paper.

Let A be the set of agents and define a *disequilibrium allocation* as a collection of net trades $z^a \in Z^a$ and of perceived constraints $\underline{z}^a$, $\bar{z}^a \in R^l$ such that z^a maximizes the preferences $\succsim_a$ on the set $\gamma^a = \{z \in Z^a \mid p \cdot z = 0, \ \underline{z}_h^a \leqslant z_h \leqslant \bar{z}_h^a, \ h \neq 0\}$ for each a. I say that agent a is *constrained* on market h if there exists t^a in the set $\gamma_h^a = \{z \in Z^a \mid p \cdot z = 0, \ \underline{z}_k^a \leqslant z_k \leqslant \bar{z}_k^a, \ k \neq 0, h\}$ such that $t^a \succ_a z^a$.

Definition. *A K-allocation is a disequilibrium allocation $(z^a, \underline{z}^a, \bar{z}^a)$ such that, for every $h \neq 0$,*

(i) *either $0 \leqslant z_h^a < t_h^a$ for all a who are constrained on market h and all $t^a \in \gamma_h^a$ such that $t^a \succ_a z^a$;*

(ii) *or $t_h^a < z_h^a \leqslant 0$ for all a who are constrained on market h and all $t^a \in \gamma_h^a$ such that $t^a \succ_a z^a$.*

It is straightforward to check that a Drèze equilibrium is a K-allocation. On the other hand, a Benassy equilibrium defines a final allocation and perceived constraints which satisfy the properties of a K-allocation when the preferences $\succsim_a$ are strictly convex (Lemma 3).

The following assumptions apply throughout the remainder of this paper:

(a) Z^a is convex;

(b) the preferences $\succsim_a$ are strictly convex.

The assumption of *strict* convexity is made to avoid unnecessary technical complications and to simplify the exposition.

III. Efficiency[1]

It is natural to ask whether a K-allocation displays any optimality property. It is clear that, if we wish a K-allocation to be optimal in the Pareto sense, we have to restrict ourselves to trades that satisfy the budget constraint $p \cdot z = 0$, i.e. to admissible trades. The following typical example shows, however, that a K-allocation need not be Pareto optimal among the class of admissible allocations if we allow the consumers, when recontracting, to trade simultaneously on all markets; see Benassy (1975), Malinvaud & Younès (1975) and Younès (1975).

Consider an exchange economy with three commodities $(l = 2)$, and two consumers i and j. Assume that there exists a K-allocation where there is an excess effective supply of commodity 1 as well as fo commodity 2, and where consumer i is a demander of commodity 1 and a supplier of commodity 2, while the situation is reversed for consumer j. The situation thus described is similar, although the analogy should not be pushed too far, to Keynesian unemployment, where there is an excess supply both on the labor market and on the market for output.

Such a situation is described in Fig. 2, which is drawn in the plane of admissible allocations. More precisely, a point in the diagram represents a net trade z for consumer i satisfying the budget constraint $p \cdot z = 0$, the point 0 describing the no-trade position. Such trade can be decomposed into two elementary trades $z_1 t^i(1)$ and $z_2 t^i(2)$ where $t^i(1) = (-p_1/p_0, 1, 0)$ and $t^i(2) = (-p_2/p_0, 0, 1)$ stand for a transaction of one unit of good 1 (or good 2) against money at ruling prices. Consumer i's preferences among trades satisfying the budget constraint are represented by indifference curves such as S^i, the most preferred point being D^i. A similar representation holds for consumer j, the elementary transactions $t^j(1)$ and $t^j(2)$ being described by vectors opposite to $t^i(1)$ and $t^i(2)$, respectively. It follows that, ignoring boundary conditions, an admissible allocation is represented by a point on the plane.

The point K is intended to describe a K-allocation where there is an excess supply on both markets. Owing to a lack of demand by consumer j, consumer i perceives a binding constraint $z_2^i \geqslant \bar{z}_2^i$ on his supply of commodity 2, which

---

[1] The material in this and the next sections is based on Grandmont, Laroque & Younès (1975).

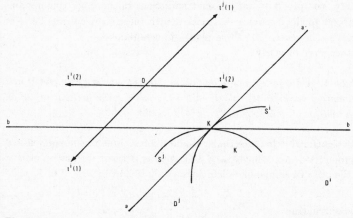

Fig. 2

is represented by the line aa'. Faced with this constraint, his most preferred point becomes K. Similarly, consumer j faces a constraint $z_1^j \geqslant \bar{z}_1^j$ on his supply of commodity 1, which is described by the line bb'.

It is clear from this picture that K is not efficient in the class of admissible allocations, since both traders can be better off by moving to K'. Such a move involves a recontracting process which takes place simultaneously on all markets. The stories usually told to explain the stability of short-run Keynesian unemployment rely heavily, however, on the role of money as a medium of exchange. For instance, it is said that any attempt by the workers to improve their position by trading labor against money cannot be succesful, for the firms take as given the constraint they perceive on their supply of output, and are thus unwilling to demand more labor.

This kind of argument rests on the assumption that the recontracting process takes place market by market. It can easily be transposed in the diagram. Suppose that the consumers try to improve their position by treading commodity 1 against money. If consumer i does not perceive the potential effect of such a move on the constraint he faces on his supply of commodity 2, he will not want to move away from K. This allocation will thus be stable.

This example suggests that we have to restrict the recontracting process to take place on a single market at a time.

Definition. *A disequilibrium allocation* $(z^a, \underline{z}^a, \bar{z}^a)$ *is efficient market by market if there is no commodity* $h \neq 0$, *and no collection of admissible trades* $t^a \in \gamma_h^a$, $a \in A$, *such that* $\sum_{a \in A} t_h^a = 0$ *and* $t^a \succsim_a z^a$ *for all* a, *with strict preference for some* a.

Note that when the agents recontract by exchanging commodity h among themselves, they ignore the quantitative constraints associated with that commodity, but plan to modify their transactions in the other commodities $k \neq h$, subject to the constraints associated with these commodities. There is no guarantee, however, that these plans are compatible.

It is then easy to verify:

Proposition 1. *A disequilibrium allocation is efficient market by market if and only if for every market h, $(t_h^a - z_h^a)(t_h^b - z_h^b) > 0$ for all a, b who are constrained on market h and for all $t^a \in \gamma_h^a$, $t^a \succ_a z^a$, $t^b \in \gamma_h^b$, $t^b \succ_b z^b$.*

It is straightforward to check that a K-allocation satisfies the property stated in the proposition. Accordingly, a K-allocation is efficient market by market among the class of admissible allocations.

IV. Recontracting

In the preceding section we characterized disequilibrium allocations that are efficient market by market. We now investigate the connection between K-allocations and the set of disequilibrium allocations that cannot be improved upon, or "blocked", by coalitions. Our goal is to show that, with a proper definition of blocking, these two sets tend to coincide when the number of agents is large, and when each of them is negligible compared to the size of the economy.

A simple example may help to understand the need for such a study. Assume that there are two commodities ($l = 1$) and two consumers i and j. An allocation can be described by a point in the Edgeworth box as in Fig. 3. Then w is the initial allocation and AB is the set of admissible allocations. There is a unique K-allocation which is described by the point D^i. There are, however, many other allocations which appear as plausible. Admissible allocations outside the segment $D^i D^j$ are unlikely to be observed since they are not efficient among the class of admissible allocations. On the other hand, any allocation represented by a point in the segment $D^i D^j$ in Fig. 3a and in the segment $D^i C$ in Fig. 3b, appears to be "stable" in the sense that any move from it (prices being given) would hurt at least one of the consumers.

This example points to the need for an argument explaining why a K-allocation is likely to be observed. The goal of this section is to show that what appears to be involved is some kind of recontracting process at given prices which makes a K-allocation the only "stable" outcome in large economies.

By analogy with traditional study of the core, and in view of the restrictions that we imposed on the recontracting process in the previous section, it might be tempting to say that a disequilibrium allocation $(z^a, \underline{z}^a, \bar{z}^a)$ is stable if there is no coalition S of consumers, no commodity $h \neq 0$ and no collection of admissible net trades $t^a \in \gamma_h^a$, $a \in S$ such that (i) $\sum_{a \in S} t_h^a = 0$, and (ii) $t^a \succsim_a z^a$ for all a in S, with strict preference for some member of S. The relationships

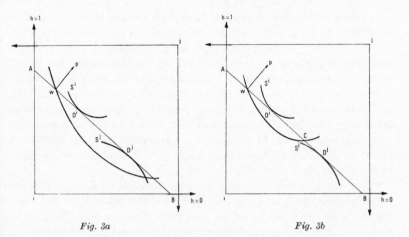

Fig. 3a   Fig. 3b

between the set of stable disequilibrium allocations and the set of K-allocations could then be studied. The following example shows, however, that with such a definition, a K-allocation would not in general be stable. Indeed, in many cases, there would be no stable disequilibrium allocation.

Consider an economy with two commodities $(l=1)$ and three consumers. Assume that in the absence of any perceived quantitative signal, consumer 1 is willing to supply, say, 20 units of commodity 1, while each of the other consumers wishes to demand 30 units of commodity 1. There is an excess demand of commodity 1. A Keynesian equilibrium is thus described by an allocation where consumer 1 actually delivers 20 units of commodity 1 to the other agents, while consumers 2 and 3 receive, respectively, z^2 and z^3 units of commodity 1, where $(z^2, z^3) \geqslant 0$ and $z^2 + z^3 = 20$. There are many such allocations, but none of them is stable if we adopt the definition presented so far. For if, say, $z^2 < 20$, then consumers 1 and 2 can redistribute their endowments among themselves so as to make consumer 2 better off without making consumer 1 worse off. The origin of this phenomenon is the fact that so far we have allowed too much competition among the traders who are actually rationed at a Keynesian equilibrium (here consumers 2 and 3). The fact that a Keynesian allocation is not in general stable in such a case means that this kind of competition is in general incompatible with the assumption of price rigidities; in the example it would presumably lead to a rise in the price of commodity 1.

This phenomenon can be avoided by requiring that a coalition, when recontracting, must improve the position of *every* member of the coalition. However, we would not need this additional requirement for the universal coalition (the set of all consumers) since the phenomenon cannot occur in such a case. It might thus be tempting to say that a disequilibrium allocation

$(z^a, \underline{z}^a, \bar{z}^a)$ is stable if it is efficient market by market, and if there is no coalition S, no commodity $h \neq 0$, and no collection of admissible trades $t^a \in \gamma_h^a$. $a \in S$, such that $\sum_{a \in S} z_h^a = 0$ and $t^a \succ_a z^a$ for all members of S. With such a definition, it can be shown that a K-allocation is always stable. But the set of stable allocations is in general much larger than the set of K-allocations, even in large economies. As a matter of fact, it can be shown that with this definition, the set of stable allocations coincides in large economies with the set of disequilibrium allocations which are efficient market by market and such that only one side of the market is constrained. But the condition of voluntary exchange may not be verified; some agents may be forced to exchange more than they wish.

I will restrict myself to illustrating these points by looking at a simple example.[1] There are two commodities $(l = 1)$ and two types of agents i and j. For the sake of simplicity, assume that there is a continuum of agents of each type. If we look only at allocations which do not discriminate among traders of the same type, then an allocation can again be described by a point in the Edgeworth box as in Fig. 3. Consider an allocation described by a point P in the segment $D^i D^j$ which differs from D^i and D^j. Let $\tilde{z}_1^i < 0$ and $\tilde{z}_1^j > 0$ be the Walrasian supply and demand for commodity 1 of the consumers of types i and j, respectively. There exist $\alpha_i > 0$, $\alpha_j > 0$ with $\alpha_i + \alpha_j = 1$ such that $\alpha_i \tilde{z}_1^i + \alpha_j \tilde{z}_1^j = 0$. If we consider a coalition S composed of a proportion α_i of consumers of type i and a proportion α_j of consumers of type j, it is possible for every member of S to achieve his most preferred trade and therefore to improve his position compared to the allocation represented by P. On the other hand, if we consider the K-allocation represented by D^i, then no coalition can improve the position of all its members, for such a coalition should be exclusively composed of consumers of type j. Similar reasoning shows that the allocation described by D^j would be stable with the definition presented so far, as long as the trade wD^j does not make the traders of type i worse off as compared to their initial endowment. Therefore, with the definition presented so far, the set of stable allocations is described by the points D^i and D^j in the case of Fig. 3a and reduces to the K-allocation D^i in Fig. 3b.

If we wish to eliminate the allocations such as D^j where, on some market h, all the buyers do realize their plans although there is an excess demand, we will clearly have to allow more coalitions to recontract out than was permitted in the last definition. In doing so, we will have to present a concept which captures the idea that when there is an excess demand on some market, the sellers are somewhat more powerful than the buyers. It turns out that this goal can be achieved by borrowing some features of the definition of a bargaining set; see Aumann & Maschler (1964).

Consider a disequilibrium allocation $(z^a, \underline{z}^a, \bar{z}^a)$. Let A be the set of agents and

---

[1] For details, see Grandmont, Laroque & Younès (1975).

let S be a coalition of consumers who wish to recontract out on some market h. There are several possibilities. First, it may be possible for the coalition S to find t^a in γ_h^a for all $a \in S$, such that $\sum_{a \in S} t_h^a = 0$, so as to improve the situation of every member of S. Then we assume that the allocation will be blocked by S, no matter what the complementary coalition $A \backslash S$ does. But the coalition S may need the help of some disjoint subset of traders T in order to achieve its goal. That is, the coalition S has to find a collection of net trades t^a which belong to γ_h^a for all a in SUT, such that $\sum_{a \in SUT} t_h^a = 0$, $t^a \succ_a z^a$ for all a in S and $t^a \sim_a z^a$ for all a in T. We saw at the beginning of this section that a K-allocation is not in general stable if we always allow such coalitions to block. It seems natural, however, to assume that this coalition will indeed block if no member of T faces an equivalent, or better proposal made by the complementary coalition $U = A \backslash (SUT)$. This will be the case if U is empty, which means that an allocation which is not efficient market by market is blocked. If U is not empty, the allocation will be blocked if for every $V = u \cup T'$, where T' is an arbitrary nonempty subset of T, there is no collection of trades s^a which belong to γ_h^a for all a in V such that $\sum_{a \in V} s_h^a = 0$ and $s^a \succ_a z^a$ for all members of V.

If we go back to the example described in Fig. 3, we find that this concept of blocking seems to succeed in capturing the dissymmetry between sellers and buyers when there is an excess demand. Let us assume again for simplicity that there is a continuum of agents of each type i and j. At the allocation represented by D^j, all sellers of commodity 1 are compelled to sell more than they intended. But they can all achieve their most preferred trade wD^i by exchanging with only a part of the set of the buyers, say T. The buyers who are left out cannot make an equivalent proposal to the members of T. The allocation represented by D^j is blocked. On the other hand, at the K-allocation described by D^i, the buyers are forced to buy less than they intended. It is true that a part S of the buyers can achieve the planned trade wD^j by exchanging with all the sellers. But in this case, the buyers who are left out can make an equivalent proposal to part of the sellers.

We shall say that a disequilibrium allocation is stable if no coalition S can block it on some market h, in the sense of the foregoing definition. Then, one can show:

Proposition 2. *In a large economy described by a continuum of agents with no atom, the set of stable allocations and the set of K-allocations coincide.*

References

Aumann, R. J. & Maschler, M.: The bargaining set for cooperative games. In M. Dresher, L. S. Shapley, A. W. Tucker (Eds.), *Advances in game theory.* Annals of Mathematical Studies, 52, Princeton University Press, 1964.

Barro, R. J. & Grossman, H. I.: A general disequilibrium model of income and employment. *American Economic Review*, March 1971.

Barro, R. J. & Grossman, H. I.: Suppressed inflation and the supply multiplier. *Review of Economic Studies*, January 1974.

Barro, R. J. & Grossman, H. I.: *Money, employment and inflation*. 1976.

Benassy, J. P.: Disequilibrium theory. Unpublished Ph.D. Thesis. Working Paper no. 185, CRMS, U.C. Berkeley, 1973.

Benassy, J. P.: A neokeynesian model of price and quantity determination in disequilibrium. CEPREMAP, to appear in Schwödiauer G. (Ed.), *Equilibrium and disequlibrium in economic theory*. Proceedings of a Conference held in Vienna, July 1974.

Benassy, J. P.: Neokeynesian disequilibrium theory in a monetary economy. *Review of Economic Studies*, 1975.

Benassy, J. P.: Effective demand, quantity signals and decision theory. CEPREMAP Paris, 1976.

Boehm, V. & Levine, J. P.: Temporary equilibria with quantity rationing. CORE D.P., 1976.

Clower, R. W.: The Keynesian counterrevolution: A theoretical appraisal. In F. H. Hahn and F. P. R. Brechling (Eds.), *The theory of interest rates*. Macmillan, 1965.

Drèze, J.: Existence of an exchange equilibrium under price rigidities. *International Economic Review*, 1975.

Grandmont, J. M.: Temporary general equilibrium theory. Project on Efficiency of Economic Systems, Harvard University, to appear in *Econometrica*. 1975.

Grandmont, J. M., Laroque, G. & Younès, Y.: Disequilibrium allocations and recontracting, IMSSS Technical Report, Stanford University, to appear in *Journal of Economic Theory*. 1975.

Grossman, H. I.: Money, interest and prices in market disequilibrium. *Journal of Political Economy*, 1971.

Grossman, H. I.: A choice-theoretic model

of an income investment accelerator. *American Economic Review*, 1972.

Hahn, F. H.: On non-Walrasian equilibria. Mimeo. 1975.

Hahn, F. H. & Negishi, T.: A theorem on non-tâtonnem entstability. *Econometrica*, 1962.

Heller, W. P. & Starr, R. M.: Unemployment equilibrium with rational expectations. IMSSS Working Paper, Stanford University, 1976.

Hildenbrand, K. & Hildenbrand, W.: On Malinvaud's reconsideration of the theory of unemployment. University of Bonn, 1976.

Leijonhufvud, A.: *On Keynesian economics and the economics of Keynes*. Oxford University Press, 1968.

Malinvaud, E.: *The theory of unemployment reconsidered*. Yrjo Lectures at the University of Helsinki, Basil Blackwell, Oxford, 1976.

Malinvaud, E. & Younès, Y.: Une nouvelle formulation générale pour l'étude des fondements microéconomiques de la macroéconomie. INSEE and CEPREMAP, Paris, 1974.

Malinvaud, E. & Younès, Y.: A new formulation for the microeconomic foundations of macroeconomics, S'Agaro, Spain, April 1975.

Negishi, T.: Existence of an underemployment equilibrium. To appear in G. Schwödiauer (Ed.), *Equilibrium and disequilibrium in economic theory*. Proceedings of a Conference held in Vienna, 1974.

Younès, Y.: Sur une notion d'equilibre utilisable dans le cas où les agents économiques ne sont pas assurés de la compatibilité de leurs plans. Contribution to the Seminaire Roy-Malinvaud, January 1970a.

Younès, Y.: Sur les notions d'equilibre et de déséquilibre utilisées dans les modèles décrivant l'évolution d'une économie capitaliste. CEPREMAP, Paris, 1970b.

Younès, Y.: On the role of money in the process of exchange and the existence of a non-Walrasian equilibrium. *Review of Economic Studies*, 1975.

RISK SHIFTING AND RELIABILITY IN LABOR MARKETS

Herschel I. Grossman

Brown University, Providence, Rhode Island, USA

Abstract

This paper analyzes the allocation of risk which is associated with variations in the value of aggregate output in a context of differences in worker and firm attitudes to risk. The analysis emphasizes two factors—limited firm risk-absorbing capacity and worker unreliability—which make it infeasible for risk-neutral firms to relieve risk-averse workers of all risk. The main ideas are that the limitation on current wage payments imposed by the value of current output implies that firms generally cannot guarantee their workers a stable consumption stream and that firms generally earn rents in their risk-absorbing role. In addition, differences among workers in their reputation for reliability, which relate to their behavior when the value of output is high, produce differences in the terms at which they can obtain consumption when the value of output is low. Specifically, workers of unproven reliability obtain less consumption in bad states of nature and, unless they plan to be unreliable, have lower current expected utility than workers of proven reliability. Those workers who earn reputations for reliability tend to be those who are relatively more risk averse and those who belong to groups which have a relatively good record for reliability.

I. Introduction

A number of recent contributions to the literature have analyzed risk-sharing arrangements between employers and employees. These papers develop what can be denoted as a Knightian view of the nature of the entrepreneur and the firm—see Knight (1921). In this view, certain individuals, either because they are intrinsically less timid or because they have substantial wealth which facilitates asset diversification, exhibit less risk-averse behavior than the average person. The equilibrium structure of a market economy finds these individuals specializing in the entrepreneurial role, forming firms, and employing labor services. These recent papers show how this systematic difference between firms and their workers with regard to risk aversion can

---

* The U.S. Department of Labor (ASPER) and the National Science Foundation have supported this research. I have received significant assistance from John Kennan and Harl Ryder. I presented an earlier version of this paper at the Econometric Society Summer Meeting, Madison, June, 1976.

lead to long-term commitments in which the firms absorb risk that would otherwise be borne by the workers.

One subset of these recent contributions—see, for example, Stiglitz (1974), Freeman (1975), and Shavell (1976)—has focused primarily on the question of how a competitive market determines the allocation of risk that is associated with variations in the value of output.[1] This analysis begins with the basic assertion, which also is the point of departure for the present discussion, that if firms are risk neutral, if the relevant stochastic variables are wholly exogenous, and if both firms and workers have identical beliefs about the probability distributions of these stochastic variables, a payment schedule which provides the workers with a riskless consumption stream describes a Pareto optimal competitive equilibrium. Under these assumptions, all relevant risk is shifted from the workers, who are averse to risk, to the firms, who are not averse to risk.

The Stiglitz, Freeman, and Shavell papers investigate various ways to relax these assumptions and generate incomplete risk shifting. Shavell, for example, allows for universal risk aversion and interpersonal differences in the intensity of risk aversion, in beliefs about stochastic elements, and in outside income services. Stiglitz and Freeman, in contrast, focus on complications involving the enforceability of employment agreements. Stiglitz considers the possibility that worker effort responds to payment incentives, which makes output per worker partly endogenous. In this case, the optimal payments schedule takes into account the trade-off between cost of payment incentives and cost of monitoring labor inputs. Freeman assumes that the perceived distribution of each worker's output becomes more concentrated as a result of past performance and that as a worker approaches retirement he would not comply with an agreement requiring him to work for less than his expected marginal product. In this case, a viable payment schedule must reward those workers who turn out to be more productive.

The main objective of the present paper is to explore two other phenomena that restrict the feasibility of risk-shifting arrangements and that seem to have fundamental empirical relevance for labor markets. The first phenomenon is the limited capacity of entrepreneurs to absorb the risk of low values of worker output. This problem is especially relevant in the labor-market context because variations in the value of output are likely to be highly correlated across individuals and to present risks that are economy wide and nondiversifiable. The nature of these risks means that relatively

---

[1] Another subset of recent contributions—see, for example, Azariadis (1975), Baily (1974), Gordon (1974), and Grossman (1975)—has attempted to deal with the interaction between the determination of production, the rationing of employment, and the sharing of risk associated with cyclical macroeconomic fluctuations. The scope of the present paper does not extend to these considerations, but the present analysis should help to provide a better foundation for tackling these problems. For an illustration of the development of the present approach in this direction, see Grossman (June, 1977).

risk-indifferent behavior by the firms in this context depends on the preferences of their owners and not on the ability of either the firms or their
owners to diversify their assets. This situation differs from the sharing of
diversiable risks, such as insurance for accident losses, which allow approximately complete risk pooling.

To highlight the phenomenon of limited risk-absorbing capacity, the present
discussion focuses on variations in the value of output that are perfectly
correlated across workers. The analysis reveals that, if the number of workers
per firm is large enough and the worst possible state of nature involves a low
enough value of output per capita, firms cannot relieve all of their workers
of all risk by guaranteeing all of them a constant consumption stream in all
states of nature. If the probability is positive that such a constraint on
firm risk-absorbing capacity will be binding, the shifting of risk from the
workers to the firms is necessarily incomplete and the implied scarcity of
risk-absorbing capacity enables the entrepreneurs to earn rents in their risk-
absorbing role.

The second phenomenon that limits the feasibility of risk-shifting arrangements is the possibility of default on employment agreements. The general
problem here is that in any arrangement in which the schedule of contingent
outcomes is motivated by optimal risk sharing, although both parties can
improve their expected outcomes by making the arrangement, one of the
parties usually will regret the actual outcome. In other words, one of the
parties usually will find that his actual outcome would be better if he were
not bound by the agreement. Specifically, when the value of a worker's output
actually turns out to be higher than the agreed wage payment, the worker
would be better off in the short run if he did not comply with this agreement
to work for this wage. In such good states of nature, he could take advantage
of the short-run availability of more lucrative alternative opportunities by
quitting his job or demanding a temporary wage increase.[1]

The discussion which follows uses the term "reliability" to refer to a worker's
willingness to forego short-run gains in order to comply with an existing
risk-shifting agreement. Note that unreliability only involves quitting or
threatening to quit when the value of the output exceeds the agreed wage
payment. No stigma attaches to changing jobs in bad states of nature. Some
arrangements for risk sharing, such as insurance for accident losses, effectively
avoid the specific problem of unreliability. However, similar solutions are not
feasible in the context of labor markets. For example, employment agreements
could require the worker initially to pay a deposit, like a premium for an
insurance policy, equal to the excess of the value of his output over his wage
in the best state of nature. To some extent, such arrangements actually exist

---

[1] For an employer, the analogous noncompliant behavior would involve temporarily
cutting wages to take advantage of the short-run availability of cheaper substitute labor
in the bad state of nature. The analysis below abstracts from such employer behavior.

in the form of deferred compensation schemes, such as nonvested pension plans. However, the utility cost to workers of such schemes is apparently sufficient to preclude arrangements that would effectively guarantee worker reliability.[1]

Another possible solution would be legal enforcement of employment agreements. However, this option is not practical because of both the sub-jective-motivation aspect of labor services and the illegality of involuntary servitude. Given these factors, employment agreements are often tacit or implicit rather than written or explicit and their viability requires extra-legal incentives for compliance.

The most important incentive of this type is probably the value of a good reputation for reliability. In the long run, both workers and firms benefit from being able to enter into risk-shifting agreements, but a record of non-compliance reduces an individual's ability to find contractual partners at favorable terms. Two important assumptions in the model developed below are that individual workers differ both in their actual reliability and in their reputations for reliability and that the correlation between individual reputa-tions and individual behavior is positive but less than perfect.

The key implication of these assumptions is that firms cannot determine the reliability of individual workers with complete accuracy on the basis of reputation. Consequently, firms face an "adverse-selection" problem.[2] Specifi-

---

[1] Salop & Salop (1976) analyze a model in which a deferred compensation scheme induces self-selection of workers according to their exogenously determined quit propensities and enables firms to eliminate turnover costs associated with firm-specific training. However, their model assumes that workers can borrow at the same interest rate that firms use to discount future profits. An analysis of deferred-compensation schemes incorporating more realistic assumptions about the cost to workers of deferred compensation would be a useful extension of the present analysis.

[2] The analysis of adverse selection developed in the present paper differs in a number of ways from the recent ambitious treatment by Rothschild & Stiglitz (1976). First, R & S focus on accident insurance and the adverse-selection problem results in their model from differences in accident probabilities. In the present context, a corresponding situation, from which the analysis abstracts, would be interpersonal differences in the distribution of the value of output. At the same time, R & S avoid the problem of differences in reliability by treating insurance premiums as prepaid. However, this difference in the source of the adverse-selection problem does not seem in itself to produce any crucial differences in the implications of the models. Second, R & S consider classes of individuals with accident probabilities which are different but less than unity. As a result, their model allows the possibility of a separating equilibrium in which these different classes buy different insurance policies. In contrast, in the present context individuals are either reliable or unreliable with probability one, a fact which precludes an analogous separating equilibrium. Third, R & S do not consider that rational insurer behavior would be to refuse to sell insurance on unprofitable terms to any individual who was foolish enough to reveal himself by his expressed demand for insurance to have a high accident probability. Consequently, in the R & S model, such individuals have no reason to dissemble their characteristics, and, as a result, a pooling equilibrium cannot exist. In contrast, in the present analysis, all workers, when entering into risk-shifting agreements, act as if they were planning to behave reliably, because to reveal themselves at this stage to be unreliable would cause firms to refuse to hire them. This dissembling behavior produces a pooling equilibrium. For an extended discussion of these general issues involving the theory of adverse selection, see Grossman (February, 1977). It is also worth noting, regarding assumptions not directly related to adverse selectrion, that R & S abstract from any effective limitation on insurers' risk-absorbing capacity and that R & S do not consider the possible accumulation of evidence on individual accident probabilities.

cally, risk-shifting arrangements, whose terms both are attractive to workers who are actually reliable and would be profitable for firms if they could limit participation to these reliable workers, can turn out to be unprofitable when workers who are actually unreliable also enroll. In addition, because firms prefer to hire reliable workers and because firms can discriminate among individual workers with partial accuracy on the basis of reputation, a reputation for reliability is valuable. As a result, in deciding whether or not to behave reliably, workers face an investment problem. Specifically, in good states of nature, a worker's incentive to behave reliably depends on a weighing of the foregone short-run gains against the long-run value of the resulting retention and enhancement of his reputation for reliability. Over time, the way that different workers solve this investment problem can enable firms to classify workers according to their probable future reliability.[1]

In what follows, Section II describes a specific analytical framework. Sections III and IV analyze how phenomena of limited risk-absorbing capacity and possible worker unreliability affect the determination of risk-shifting arrangements in a competitive market. Section V discusses the nature of the investment process by which a worker obtains a reputation for reliability. Finally, Section VI summarizes the main results.

II. Analytical Framework

Consider the following simple economy: There are three large classes of identical individuals, which differ only in their attitudes to risk and in their reputations for reliability, in the sense defined above. One large class of identical individuals behaves as if they were risk neutral. Specifically, their utility is a linear function of consumption. Thus, they are indifferent between a constant consumption stream and a fluctuating consumption stream that has the same average value. In addition, as entrepreneurs, the role which the theory implies that only they play, the individuals in this class have a deserved reputation for complete reliability. This assumption means that employers never fail to comply with the risk-shifting agreements which they have made.

The second large class of individuals exhibits a positive degree of risk aversion. Specifically, their utility is a concave function of consumption. Thus, they prefer a constant consumption stream to a fluctuating stream that has the same average value. In addition, as employees, the role which the theory implies that they play, the individuals in this class also have proven

---

[1] This way of separating the workers based on experience after they are employed becomes especially important because, as indicated in the preceding footnote, the assumptions of the model preclude the possibility of separating the workers before they become employed. A number of recent contributions—see, for example, Spence (1973)—have focused on a similar procedure which uses investment in education prior to employment as a signaling device to separate workers of differing productivities.

their reliability. The number of individuals in this second class is R times the number of individuals in the risk-neutral class.

The third large class of individuals also exhibits a positive degree of risk aversion. However, these individuals, who can also play the role of employees, have not as yet proven themselves to be reliable. The number of individuals in this third class is U times the number of individuals in the risk-neutral class.

This class of unproven individuals consists of two subclasses. One subclass actually is completely reliable. The number of individuals in this subclass is $(1-q)U$ times the number of individuals in the risk-neutral class. The other subclass actually is completely unreliable. The number of individuals in this subclass is qU times the number of individuals in the risk-neutral class. Although the firms do not know which unproven individuals are in which of these subclasses, they do know the number of individuals in each subclass. The discussion will eventually consider the possible causes of this difference in the actual reliability of these two subclasses of unproven individuals. For the moment, however, let us take these differences as given, but also note that these two subclasses need not have the same degree of risk aversion.

This framework of three classes of individuals is a convenient simplification of a more general analysis that would allow for many classes of unproven individuals that differ in the fraction of individuals who are actually unreliable. The results in section IV below extend readily to cover this general case.[1]

In order to focus on the importance of risk shifting, the analysis ignores the technological aspects of the organization of production. Such factors as the advantages of team production, firm-specific human capital, costs of adjusting employment, and mobility costs surely influence both the organization of production and the form of optimal long-term agreements between firms and workers. However, the present analysis considers only the role played by firms in absorbing risk that their employees otherwise would bear. Specifically, the analysis assumes that each individual in the economy would be equally productive whether he chose to be an independent producer, an employer, or an employee. In other words, the assumed technology makes production solely an independent activity. In addition, the analysis abstracts from interpersonal differences in productivity. Thus, the value of output across individuals is perfectly correlated.

The value of per capita output, denoted by X, is the product of number of units of output per capita and, if this output is not directly consumed, the exchange ratio between consumption goods and produced output in the

---

[1] A more ambitious extension, which would become interesting in a context involving many states of nature, would be to analyze explicitly individuals who are partially unreliable in the sense that they would quit only if the short-run gains exceeded a certain positive amount.

world market.[1] Either or both of the factors in this product can be subject to variation. Specifically, assume that the actual value of X is determined at periodic intervals by serially independent drawings from an exogenously determined population. The interval between these drawings defines a unit of time. The population of X is such that

$$X = \begin{cases} X_1 \text{ with probability } \alpha_1 \\ X_2 \text{ with probability } \alpha_2, \end{cases}$$

where $X_2 > X_1 \geqslant 0$, $\alpha_1 + \alpha_2 = 1$, and $0 < \alpha_1 < 1$. Thus, X_2 characterizes a good state of nature and X_1 characterizes a bad state of nature. The expected value of per capita output is

$$\alpha_1 X_1 + \alpha_2 X_2.$$

As is discussed below, the analysis readily generalizes to a situation of many states of nature.

The analysis also assumes that consumption goods and produced output are the only commodities in the economy—specifically, there are no investment goods—and neither consumption goods nor produced output are storable. These assumptions imply that, in aggregate, current consumption is equal to the value of current output, and that, in aggregate, the economy cannot smooth out its consumption stream by varying either its accumulation of investment goods or its commodity inventories. Allowing for either investment goods or commodity inventories would make the analysis both more realistic and more complex, but as is noted below, would not seem to change the main conclusions regarding the market for risk-shifting arrangements.

Another convenient simplification is that individuals have no alternative uses, such as direct production of consumption goods or leisure activities, to which to devote their time. This assumption, together with the assumption that production is an independent activity, implies that the level of marketable output is independent of the price of output and the demand for output. This formulation also enables the analysis to avoid treating explicitly the possibility of varying hours of work. Allowing for either a positive alternative cost of time or a more complex production technology would not be difficult, but the present abstractions permit the analysis to concentrate on the relation between risk shifting and the arrangements by which individuals dispose of their output and receive claims to consumption goods.

III. The Problem of Limited Risk-Absorbing Capacity

One option that is available to each individual, and that sets a minimum acceptable level of expected utility for each individual, is to be an independent

---

[1] This exchange ratio represents what is usually called the terms of trade. Thus, all variations in x involve "real" disturbances. It is not clear to what extent the analysis in this paper would be applicable to disturbances which are identifiable as purely "monetary".

producer, who sells his output directly on the world market and has no dealings with other producers. If an individual were an independent producer, his actual consumption would be equal to either X_1 or X_2. Thus, all independent producers would have the same, equally risky, consumption stream.

Consider, for the moment, only the two classes of individuals with reputations for complete reliability. A proposition that we can easily establish is that the assumed difference between the risk attitudes of these two classes will generate a market equilibrium in which no individual in these classes would choose to be an independent producer. This market equilibrium would involve an arrangement for shifting risk associated with the stochastic value of per capita output from the individuals in the risk-averse class to the individuals in the risk-neutral class. What form would this arrangement take?

The obvious device for optimal risk shifting would be for each risk-neutral individual to become an entrepreneur, who forms a firm which acts as an employer, and for each risk-averse individual to become an employee, who works for one of the firms. Under this employee–employer arrangement, each worker would contract to turn over his output to a firm rather than to sell it directly in the market, and he would contract to receive from that firm claims on consumption in the form of wage payments that would imply for him a combination of expected consumption and risk at least as desirable as he would have if he had remained self employed. This arrangement must also provide each entrepreneur with claims on consumption in the form of the net income receipts of his firm that would imply for him a level of expected consumption at least as large as he would have if he did not form a firm. The central analytical problem is to determine the specifications of the equilibrium consumption schedules for workers and entrepreneurs.

A worker consumption schedule is a vector (w_1, w_2), where $w_1(w_2)$ is the wage payment if X turns out to equal $X_1(X_2)$. An entrepreneur consumption schedule is a vector (Π_1, Π_2), where $\Pi_1(\Pi_2)$ is net income if X turns out to equal $X_1(X_2)$. Let p denote the exchange ratio at which individuals give up or receive consumption in the good state in return for consumption in the bad state. Specifically, p is the price of consumption in state one in units of consumption in state two. A value of p equal to unity would characterize an actuarially "fair" price.[1]

Each entrepreneur, when entering into employment agreements, seeks to maximize expected consumption,

$$\alpha_1 \Pi_1 + \alpha_2 \Pi_2,$$

subject to the budget constraint,

$$p\alpha_1 \Pi_1 + \alpha_2 \Pi_2 = p\alpha_1 X_1 + \alpha_2 X_2,$$

---

[1] This characterization is independent of α_1 and α_2. Note, however, that the price p corresponds to an insurance premium rate, payable in both states, of $p\alpha_1/(p\alpha_1 + \alpha_2)$ per dollar of indemnity receivable in the bad state. Thus, p equal to unity implies a premium rate equal to α_1.

and the nonnegativity constraints,

$$\Pi_1 \geqslant 0 \quad \text{and} \quad \Pi_2 \geqslant 0.$$

This maximization implies the following entrepreneurial demand schedule for consumption in state one:

$$\Pi_1 \begin{cases} = X_1 + \dfrac{\alpha_2}{\alpha_1} \dfrac{X_2}{p} & \text{for} \quad p < 1 \\[2mm] \varepsilon\left[X_1 + \dfrac{\alpha_2}{\alpha_1} \dfrac{X_2}{p},\ 0 \right] & \text{for} \quad p = 1 \\[2mm] = 0 & \text{for} \quad p > 1. \end{cases}$$

According to this demand schedule, at any value of p greater than or equal to unity, each entrepreneur is willing to reduce his consumption in the bad state to the minimum possible, which is zero. By so doing, the entrepreneurs make all of their own output available to supplement the consumption of the workers should the bad state occur.

Each worker, when entering into an employment agreement, seeks to maximize expected utility,

$$\alpha_1 u(w_1) + \alpha_2 u(w_2),$$

subject to the budget constraint,

$$p\alpha_1 w_1 + \alpha_2 w_2 = p\alpha_1 X_1 + \alpha_2 X_2,$$

and the nonnegativity constraints,

$$w_1 \geqslant X_1 \quad \text{and} \quad w_2 \geqslant 0,$$

where $u(w)$ is the worker's concave utility function. The constraint $w_1 \geqslant X_1$ rules out the possibility that these individuals might try to play the entrepreneurial role, in which they have no reputation for reliability. This maximization involves the first-order condition,

$$u'(w_1) = pu'(w_2),$$

which in turn implies the following worker demand schedule for consumption in state one:

$$w_1 = \max\left[f(p),\ X_1 \right],\ f'(p) < 0,\ f[u'(X_1)/u'(X_2)] = X_1,\ f(1) = \alpha_1 X_1 + \alpha_2 X_2.$$

According to this demand schedule, as long as p is less than ratio of the marginal utilities of X_1 and X_2, each worker desires to reduce his risk by contracting for w_1 to exceed X_1. As p decreases, his desired level of w_1 increases. If p is equal to unity, he wants w_1 to equal the average level of per capita output, which, according to his budget constraint, is equivalent to making w_1 equal to w_2 and thereby avoiding all risk.

In order to clear the market for employment agreements, the exchange ratio p must adjust to equate the total demand for consumption in state one with actual output in state one. Let p^* denote this market-clearing value of p. Assuming for simplicity that all the reliable workers have the same utility function, p^* satisfies the market-clearing condition

$$\Pi_1 + Rw_1 = (1 + R)X_1.$$

To facilitate analysis of this condition, define a price $\hat{p}$ such that

$$Rf(\hat{p}) = (1 + R)X_1.$$

The first-order condition for maximization of worker utility together with the worker budget constraint implies that $\hat{p}$ satisfies

$$u'\left(\frac{1+R}{R}X_1\right) = \hat{p}u'\left(X_2 - \hat{p}\frac{\alpha_1}{\alpha_2}\frac{X_1}{R}\right).$$

The solution of the market-clearing condition is

$$p^* = \max(1, \hat{p}).$$

Which value p^* takes depends on whether or not $\Pi_1 \geqslant 0$ is a binding constraint. Consider each of these two possible cases in turn: Case one, in which $p^* = 1$, occurs if $\hat{p} \leqslant 1$, which implies

$$Rf(1) \leqslant (1 + R)X_1,$$

or, equivalently,

$$\frac{\alpha_1 X_1 + \alpha_2 X_2}{X_1} \leqslant \frac{1+R}{R}.$$

This condition requires that the ratio of the average value of output to the value of output in the bad state and the ratio of the number of risk-averse individuals to the number of risk-neutral individuals both be sufficiently small to enable the entrepreneurs to provide the workers with a level of consumption in the bad state equal to the average value of per capita output without violating the constraint that entrepreneurial consumption must be nonnegative.

Given that this condition is satisfied, all risk is shifted to the entrepreneurs. We can easily calculate from the budget constraints that, in this case, worker consumption is a constant, independent of the state of nature, whereas entrepreneurial consumption, although nonnegative in both states of nature, is more variable than per capita output. Moreover, the expected

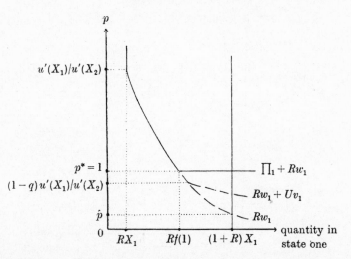

Fig. 1. Solid locus $\Pi_1 + Rw_1$ represents total demand for consumption in state one. Vertical line $(1+R)X_1$ represents total supply of consumption in state one. $Rf(1) = R(\alpha_1 X_1 + \alpha_2 X_2) < (1+R)X_1$ implies that constraint on risk-absorbing capacity is not binding. Consequently, $p^* = 1$ and $X_1 < w_1 = f(1) = \alpha_1 X_1 + \alpha_2 X_2$. Also, $p^* > (1-q)u'(X_1)/u'(X_2)$ implies that unproven workers do not participate in risk-shifting agreements, i.e., $v_1 = X_1$—see section 4.

values of worker and entrepreneurial consumption are both equal to the expected value of per capita output, as would be the case for self-employed workers.[1] In other words, workers obtain a riskless consumption pattern at no cost to themselves in terms of average consumption. Figure 1 illustrates an example of this case.

Case two, in which $p^* = \hat{p} > 1$, occurs if

$$Rf(1) > (1+R)X_1,$$

or, equivalently,

$$\frac{\alpha_1 X_1 + \alpha_2 X_2}{X_1} > \frac{1+R}{R}.$$

Under these conditions, at p equal to unity, the constraint that Π_1 must be nonnegative would be binding. Consequently, to clear the market, p must be sufficiently greater than unity to reduce worker demands for consumption in state one to the level of output in state one. In this case, the level of p induces

---

[1] This equality is probably not consistent with the assumption that firms are completely reliable, because it implies that a firm would lose nothing by being excluded from the market for risk-shifting agreements. A plausible restriction would have these arrangements sufficiently profitable to make it always optimal for firms to comply with the equilibrium risk-shifting agreement. The alternative outcome of p greater than unity can avoid this inconsistency.

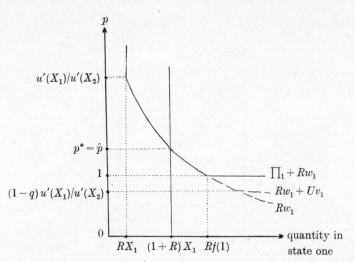

Fig. 2. $Rf(1) > (1+R)X_1$ implies that constraint on risk-absorbing capacity is binding. Consequently, $p^* = \hat{p} > 1$ and $X_1 < w_1 < f(1) = \alpha_1 X_1 + \alpha_2 X_2$. Also, $p^* > (1-q) u'(X_1)/u'(X_2)$ implies that unproven workers do not participate in risk-shifting agreements, i.e., $v_1 = X_1$—see section 4.

the entrepreneurs to consume nothing in the bad state, but even so they cannot stabilize worker consumption at the average value of output. Worker consumption in the bad state, which equals $((1+R)/R)X_1$, exceeds per capita output in the bad state, as long as X_1 is positive, but is smaller than worker consumption in the good state. Moreover, the scarcity of risk-absorbing capacity enables the entrepreneurs to earn rents. The expected value of their consumption exceeds the average value of per capita output. Consequently, workers, although they have higher expected utility than if self-employed, have to accept some reduction in their average consumption below the average value of per capita output in order to obtain a partial reduction in the riskiness of their consumption.[1] Fig. 2 illustrates an example of this case.

---

[1] An interesting extension of this analysis would be to allow for the holding of stocks of commodities which could be consumed or exchanged for consumption goods in the bad state of nature. With such stocks, the constraint on aggregate consumption in the bad state is the sum of the value of output in the bad state plus the value of existing commodity stocks. However, the key observation in this context is that, because the accumulation of commodity stocks involves foregoing consumption, it would not be optimal for the risk-averse individuals to hold stocks which are so large that, in the absence of complete risk shifting, they would not reduce their consumption in the bad state. For a derivation of this result, see, for example, the analysis by Foley & Hellwig (1975) of a related problem. This result obtains even if the holding of commodity stocks involved no storage cost, although such costs of course would reduce the optimal level of stock holding. Thus, allowing for stocks would not seem to affect the general conclusions drawn above regarding the market for risk-shifting arrangements. Nevertheless, a full analysis of the interaction between stock holding and risk sharing would present a challenging problem, which is beyond the scope of the present paper. Note also that the holding of financial assets has no role to play in the present context of aggregate real disturbances. Financial assets can provide effective cushioning of per capita consumption only for disturbances which do not impair aggregate production potential.

At this point, we can usefully consider a generalization of the analysis to allow for the possibility of many, rather than only two, states of nature. For example, let the population of X be such that

$X = X_i$ with probability α_i, where

$$i = 1 \ldots n \quad \text{and} \quad \sum_{i=1}^{n} \alpha_i = 1.$$

Index the states in order of increasing values of X, so that

$$X_1 < X_2 < \ldots < X_n.$$

This generalization presents two new analytical problems: The first problem is to determine a vector of prices for consumption in each state in (say) units of consumption in the best state, which is state n. From the preceding discussion, we infer that

$$p_1^* \geqslant p_2^* \geqslant \ldots \geqslant p_n^* = 1 \quad \text{and} \quad w_1 \leqslant w_2 \leqslant \ldots \leqslant w_n,$$

and that worker consumption is the same in all states which have the same price of consumption. We can also infer that

$$p_i^* = 1 \quad \text{and} \quad w_i = \sum_{i=1}^{n} \alpha_i X_i, \quad \text{for all} \quad i = 1 \ldots n, \quad \text{iff} \quad p_1^* = 1.$$

and that

$$p_1^* = 1 \quad \text{iff} \quad \sum_{i=1}^{n} \alpha_i X_i \leqslant \frac{1+R}{R} X_1.$$

Thus, the result still obtains that all risk is shifted to the firms, with the workers having constant consumption and the entrepreneurs earning no rents, if and only if both the ratio of the average value of output to the value of output in the worst state and the ratio of the number of workers to the number of entrepreneurs are small enough to enable the workers to consume the average level of output in the worst state.

More generally, we can derive the following result:

$$p_1^* > \ldots > p_{k-1}^* > p_k^* = \ldots = p_n^* = 1 \quad \text{and} \quad w_1 < \ldots < w_{k-1} < w_k = \ldots = w_n = \bar{w},$$

where

$$k = \min \left[i \left| \frac{\sum_{j=1}^{n} \alpha_j X_j - \sum_{j=1}^{i-1} \alpha_j p_j (w_j - X_j)}{\sum_{j=i}^{n} \alpha_j} \leqslant \frac{1+R}{R} X_i \right. \right], \quad i = 1 \ldots n,$$

and

$$\bar{w} = \frac{\displaystyle\sum_{j=k}^{n} \alpha_j X_j - \sum_{j=1}^{k-1} \alpha_j p_j (w_j - X_j)}{\displaystyle\sum_{j=k}^{n} \alpha_j}$$

This result implies that, in all states in which X is sufficiently large that the potential constraint on firm risk-absorbing capacity is not binding, the price of consumption is unity and worker consumption is constant and equal to the conditional expected value of per capita output in these states net of worker expenditure on consumption in the other (worse) states.

The second new problem is to determine which of the n states are bad states, in the sense that worker consumption in these states exceeds the value of per capita output, and which states are good states. The general result here is that

$$w_i \gtreqless X_i \quad \text{as} \quad \bar{w} \gtreqless X_i, \quad i = 1, \dots, n.$$

This relation implies that the set of good states is a subset of the set of states for which the price of consumption is unity. Thus, workers have constant consumption in the good states and they use the expected excess of output per capita over worker consumption in the good states to purchase additional consumption in the bad states, bringing consumption in the better bad states up to the same constant level and bringing consumption in the worse bad states up to the level permitted by the binding constraint on firm risk-absorbing capacity.

IV. The Problem of Unreliable Workers

The analysis so far has not taken account of the third class of individuals, who are risk averse but whose reliability is as yet unproven. Because a positive number, qU, of unproven individuals are actually unreliable, the unproven individuals cannot obtain the same schedule of wage payments as is available to the class of workers of proven reliability. However, because a positive number of unproven individuals, $(1-q)U$, are actually reliable, the firms can offer the unproven individuals a limited risk-shifting arrangement. This arrangement may or may not be sufficiently attractive to induce them to join the reliable individuals as employees of the firms.

Let us again focus on a situation of only two possible states of nature, and consider the possible participation of unproven workers in risk-shifting agreements. When dealing with the class of unproven individuals, each entrepreneur's budget constraint becomes

$$(1-q)p\alpha_1 \Pi_1 + \alpha_2 \Pi_2 = (1-q)p\alpha_1 X_1 + \alpha_2 X_2.$$

Consequently, each entrepreneur is indifferent between making risk-shifting agreements with proven reliable workers at price p and making risk-shifting agreements with unproven workers at the higher price $p/(1-q)$.

An individual worker, of course, is in the unproven class only because he has not shown himself as yet to be reliable but also has not revealed himself to be unreliable. If the firms were able to identify a particular worker as being actually unreliable, they would avoid any risk-shifting arrangement with that individual. Specifically, for an individual who is actually unreliable, any risk-shifting agreement would involve an effective price of consumption in state one of zero, because such an individual intends to quit if state two occurs. However, any individual who when entering into a risk-shifting agreement attempted to act as if he faced a zero price would identify himself as actually unreliable. Consequently, all unproven workers find it in their own best interest when entering into risk-shifting agreements to act as if they were planning to behave reliably. This strategy means that they exhibit a demand schedule for consumption in state one which has the same form as that of the proven reliable workers. Any unproven worker who demanded more consumption in state one than a proven reliable worker would demand at that price would reveal himself to be unreliable.[1]

Given this specification for the behavior of the unproven workers, their demand schedule for consumption in state one is

$$v_1 = \max\left[f\left(\frac{p}{1-q}\right),\, X_1\right],$$

where the vector (v_1, v_2) represents an unproven worker's consumption schedule. This demand schedule is identical to the demand schedule of the reliable workers except that an effective price of $p/(1-q)$ replaces the nominal price p. Consequently, even if p is equal unity, the effective price to unproven workers is higher than the actuarially fair price, and they do not attempt to avoid all risk by contracting for v_1 to be equal $\alpha_1 X_1 + \alpha_2 X_2$. Moreover, in order for unproven workers to enter at all into risk-shifting agreements, which provide for v_1 to exceed X_1, p and q have to be such that

$$\frac{p}{1-q} < \frac{u'(X_1)}{u'(X_2)}.$$

Although all unproven workers have the same level of consumption in the bad state, they generally do not all have the same level of consumption in

---

[1] Again, it is convenient to assume that all proven reliable workers have the same demand schedules. The discussion in section 5 below suggests that the shape of utility functions and, hence, the specification of demand schedules are unlikely to differ substantially among the reliable workers.

the good state. For those unproven workers who are actually reliable, consumption in state two satisfies the budget constraint

$$\frac{p}{1-q}\alpha_1 v_1 + \alpha_2 v_2 = \frac{p}{1-q}\alpha_1 X_1 + \alpha_2 X_2.$$

Consequently, for these workers, $v_1 > X_1$ implies $v_2 < X_2$. However, for those unproven workers who are actually unreliable, consumption in state two is simply equal to X_2.

Taking account of both proven reliable and unproven workers, total worker demand for consumption in state one is

$$Rw_1 + Uv_1 = \begin{cases} X(R+U)X_1 & \text{for} \quad p \geqslant \dfrac{u'(X_1)}{u'(X_2)} \\[2ex] Rf(p) + UX_1 & \text{for} \quad \dfrac{u'(X_1)}{u'(X_2)} > p \geqslant (1-q)\dfrac{u'(X_1)}{u'(X_2)} \\[2ex] Rf(p) + Uf\left(\dfrac{p}{1-q}\right) & \text{for} \quad p < (1-q)\dfrac{u'(X_1)}{u'(X_2)}, \end{cases}$$

and the market-clearing condition for employment agreements is

$$\Pi_1 + Rw_1 + Uv_1 = (1 + R + U)X_1.$$

Let p^{**} denote the value of p which is consistent with this market-clearing condition.

The solution of this market-clearing condition for p^{**} involves four possible cases, which differ according to whether or not the unproven workers actually participate in risk-shifting agreements and whether or not the constraint on entrepreneurial risk-absorbing capacity is binding. Either case one or case two occurs if

$$p^* = \max(1, \hat{p}) \geqslant (1-q)\frac{u'(X_1)}{u'(X_2)}.$$

According to this condition, the proportion of actually unreliable individuals in the unproven class is sufficiently large that this class would not participate in risk-shifting agreements at the price, p^*, that would clear the market for employment agreements in their absence. Consequently, in these two cases, we have v_1 equal to X_1, and the market-clearing condition reduces to

$$\Pi_1 + Rw_1 = (1 + R)X_1,$$

which was the specification analyzed in section 3 and which implies the solution

$$p^{**} = p^* = \max(1, \hat{p}).$$

Thus, cases one and two here are essentially equivalent to the two cases analyzed in section 3.

More precisely, case one, an example of which is illustrated in Fig. 1, requires both

$$1 > (1-q)\frac{u'(X_1)}{u'(X_2)} \quad \text{and} \quad \frac{\alpha_1 X_1 + \alpha_2 X_2}{X_2} \leqslant \frac{1+R}{R},$$

and implies that $p^{**} = 1$. Case two, an example of which is illustrated in Fig. 2, requires both

$$\hat{p} \geqslant (1-q)\frac{u'(X_1)}{u'(X_2)} \quad \text{and} \quad \frac{\alpha_1 X_1 + \alpha_2 X_2}{X_1} > \frac{1+R}{R},$$

and implies that $p^{**} = \hat{p} > 1$.

Either case three or case four occurs if

$$p^* = \max(1, \hat{p}) < (1-q)\frac{u'(X_1)}{u'(X_2)}.$$

According to this condition, individuals in the unproven class would desire to enter into risk-shifting agreements at the price, p^*, that would clear the market in their absence. Specifically, case three occurs if both

$$1 < (1-q)\frac{u'(X_1)}{u'(X_2)} \quad \text{and} \quad Rf(1) + Uf\left(\frac{1}{1-q}\right) \leqslant (1+R+U)X_1.$$

This latter condition means that, at p equal to unity, the entrepreneurs can provide

$$w_1 = \alpha_1 X_1 + \alpha_2 X_2 \quad \text{and} \quad X_1 < v_1 = f\left(\frac{1}{1-q}\right) < \alpha_1 X_1 + \alpha_2 X_2$$

without violating the constraint that Π_1 must be nonnegative. Consequently, the market-clearing condition implies

$$p^{**} = p^* = 1.$$

In case three, as in case one, proven reliable workers obtain a riskless consumption schedule, and the expected value of their consumption as well as entrepreneurial consumption are both equal to the expected value of per capita output. However, in case three, unproven workers also obtain some reduction in the riskiness of their consumption. Consequently, entrepreneurial consumption is more variable than in case one. As we can easily calculate from the budget constraint, the unproven workers who are actually reliable accept in return an expected value of consumption that is less than average per capita output. Those unproven workers who are actually unreliable achieve a

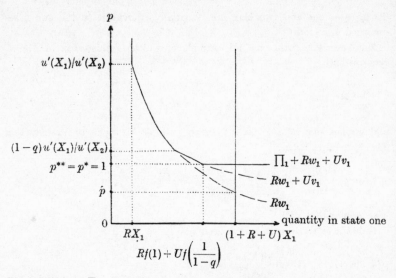

Fig. 3. Solid locus $\Pi_1 + Rw_1 + Uv_1$ represents total demand for consumption in state one. Vertical line $(1 + R + U)X_1$ represents total supply of consumption in state one. $p^* = 1 < (1-q)u'(X_1)/u'(X_2)$ implies that unproven workers participate in risk-shifting agreements. $Rf(1) + Uf(1/(1-q)) < (1 + R + U)X_1$ implies that constraint on risk-shifting capacity is not binding. Consequently, $p^{**} = p^* = 1$, $X_1 < w_1 = f(1)$, and $X_1 < v_1 = f(1/(1-q)) < f(1)$.

matching increase in the expected value of their consumption. Fig. 3 illustrates an example of this case.

Finally, case four occurs if both

$$\max(1, \hat{p}) < (1-q)\frac{u'(X_1)}{u'(X_2)} \quad \text{and} \quad Rf(1) + Uf\left(\frac{1}{1-q}\right) > (1 + R + U)X_1.$$

This latter condition means that, at p equal to unity, the constraint that Π_1 cannot be negative would be binding. Consequently, the market-clearing condition implies

$$p^{**} > p^* \geqslant 1.$$

In case four, as in case two, the entrepreneurs consume nothing in the bad state, but in return they earn rents, which make the expected value of their consumption greater than the average value of per capita output. All workers obtain a partial reduction in the riskiness of their consumption, but consumption in the bad state is larger for proven reliable workers than for unproven workers. Expected consumption is less than expected per capita output for all reliable workers, but is larger for the proven reliable workers. Those unproven workers who are actually unreliable have expected consumption greater than expected per capita output, as in case three. A distinctive

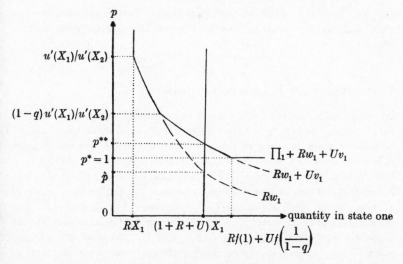

Fig. 4. $p^* < (1-q)u'(X_1)/u'(X_2)$ implies that unproven workers participate in risk-shifting agreements. $Rf(1) + Uf(1/(1-q)) > (1+R+U)X_1$ implies that constraint on risk-absorbing is binding. Consequently, $p^{**} > p^* > 1$, $X_1 < w_1 < f(1)$, and $X_1 < v_1 < f(1/(1-q)) < f(1)$.

feature of case four is that the participation of unproven workers in risk-shifting agreements causes p^{**} to be higher than p^*, which reduces the expected utility of the proven reliable workers and increases the average consumption of the entrepreneurs. Fig. 4 illustrates an example of this case.

With regard to risk-shifting characteristics, we can summarize these four cases as follows: In case one, entrepreneurs absorb all risk from the proven reliable workers, but absorb no risk from the unproven workers. In case two, entrepreneurs absorb some risk from the proven reliable workers, but again absorb no risk from the unproven workers. In case three, entrepreneurs absorb all risk from the proven reliable workers and absorb some risk from the unproven workers. In case four, entrepreneurs absorb some risk from the proven reliable workers and absorb some, but less, risk from the unproven workers.

Some important generalizations emerge from the analysis of these cases: First, in all cases consumption in the bad state is smaller for unproven workers than for proven reliable workers. Second, in all cases current expected utility is smaller for unproven workers who are actually reliable than for proven reliable workers. Third, if unproven workers participate in risk-shifting agreements, as in cases three and four, expected consumption is smaller for unproven workers who are actually reliable than for proven reliable workers. Finally, we can readily establish that these conclusions carry over to a situation of many, rather than only two, states of nature. The main new complication introduced in the multistate context is that unproven workers could participate in risk shifting for some of the bad states but not for others.[1]

V. Investment in a Reputation for Reliability

To complete the theory of risk shifting and reliability, this section sketches an investment process by which workers acquire reputations for reliability. In this discussion, it is convenient to consider the general context of many states of nature and many classes of unproven workers that differ in the fraction of workers who are apt to be unreliable in the various good states. Indexing the classes so that the higher the class the smaller the fraction of workers who are unreliable in each good state allows us to say that the higher the workers's class the better his reputation for reliability and to infer that the higher the worker's class the better the terms, i.e., the lower the price, at which he can enter into agreements for shifting risks in any bad state of nature.

The essential assumption in this section is that the classification of workers is based on an empirical regularity that the longer a worker participates reliably in risk-shifting agreements with a single firm, the less likely he is to quit at any given future opportunity. An empirical rationalization for this regularity is that a worker's length of service with a particular firm is a good proxy for the number and attractiveness of his past opportunities to quit and that the factors that determine a worker's decision whether or not to quit in a given good state are not likely to change unfavorably over time. This method of classification means that to analyze the determination of a worker's reputation for reliability we must consider the factors that determine the reliability of his actual behavior.[2]

A worker's decision not to quit when X exceeds w involves both a cost and a benefit. The cost is the foregone temporary increase in consumption. The benefit includes both the retention of an already acquired reputation for reliability and the enhancement of that reputation. The value of this benefit to a particular worker depends (1) on his existing classification, which involves his current length of service, (2) on the incremental improvement in his classification associated with an increase in his length of service, and (3) on the importance to him of the terms on which he can enter into risk-shifting

---

[1] In addition, as noted above, the multistate context suggests the possible complications that a worker could be reliable in moderately good states but unreliable in very good states and that workers could differ with regard to the best state in which they are reliable.

[2] This method also implies that the dynamics of the system require that the lowest class of workers participate in risk-shifting agreements for one or more of the bad states of nature.

agreements.[1] Differences in the first factor develop over time and both reflect and reinforce the effect of differences in the latter two factors. Differences in the latter two factors could be the result of either intrinsic differences among the workers or preconceptions by the firms regarding such differences.

As an example of an intrinsic difference, suppose that worker utility functions exhibit different degrees of risk aversion. Suppose also that the firms have no preconceptions regarding the reliability of particular workers. This absence of preconceptions means that the forms apply to each worker the same functional relation between classification and length of service. However, given the length of service, the more risk averse the worker the higher the value he puts on the benefit from retaining and enhancing his classification. Consequently, the more risk averse the worker the less apt he is to quit and, hence, the more rapidly on average he improves his classification.

As another example, suppose that the firms have a common preconception that certain workers—for example, blacks—are relatively more likely to be unreliable. Suppose, in addition, that, although this preconception might have an historical basis in fact, there is currently no correlation between this preconception and any intrinsic differences among the workers that might influence their reliability. Nevertheless, acting in accord with their preconceptions, the firms gave blacks a lower classification for a given length of service than they give other workers. This practice on the part of firms makes the value of the benefit to a black worker from retaining and enhancing his reputation for reliability less than for nonblack workers with the same length of service and the same degree of risk aversion. Consequently, although black workers are not intrinsically different, they are more apt to behave unreliably than are nonblack workers with the same length of service. Thus, the preconceptions of the firms are self confirming.

This type of equilibrium, based on intrinsically unfounded but self-confirming preconceptions, has unstable properties. Specifically, it would not survive determined experimentation by firms based on the correct hypothesis that blacks and nonblacks are not intrinsically different with regard to characteristics which influence their reliability. Nevertheless, such an equilibrium could persist for a lengthy stretch of calendar time.[2]

---

[1] As a worker nears retirement, the first and third factors move in opposite directions. His existing classification increases, while the difference in future utility associated with the terms on which he can enter into risk-shifting agreements decreases. The latter effect suggests that as he nears retirement, he would have little motivation to maintain his acquired reputation for reliability. However, at the same time, other schemes to encourage reliability, such as nonvested pension plans, probably become more effective.

[2] This example is similar to the example of a signaling equilibrium suggested by Spence (1973) in which women invest less in education than do men. Riley (1975) argues that a signaling equilibrium based on unfounded preconceptions could not survive in a competitive situation.

VI. Summary

This paper has analyzed the allocation of risk which is associated with variations in the value of aggregate output in a context of differences in worker and firm attitudes to risk. The analysis emphasizes two factors—limited firm risk-absorbing capacity and worker unreliability—that make it infeasible for risk-neutral firms to relieve risk-averse workers of all risk. A principal conclusion is that actually observed relations between firms and workers, which do include the possibility of reductions or even suspensions of wage payments, are consistent with optimal risk shifting, subject to these feasibility constraints.

The problem of limited risk-absorbing capacity reflects the limitation that the value of current output imposes on current wage payments when the value of output is low. This limitation means that firms generally cannot guarantee their workers a stable consumption stream through an agreement providing a fixed wage payment, and that firms generally earn rents in their risk-absorbing role.

The problem of worker unreliability results from the possibility that the prospect of short-run gains, when the value of output is high, can induce workers to quit their jobs. Differences among workers in their reputation for reliability, which relate to their behavior when the value of output is high, produce differences in the terms at which they can obtain consumption when the value of output is low. Specifically, workers of unproven reliability obtain less consumption in bad states of nature and, unless they plan to be unreliable, have lower current expected utility than workers of proven reliability.

The investment process by which a worker establishes his reputation for reliability requires that the worker actually behave reliably—that is, that he not quit to obtain short-run gains. The benefit from reliable behavior is greater the more risk averse is a particular worker and the more predisposed the firms are to regard a particular worker as reliable. Consequently, those workers who through long service with a single firm earn good reputations for reliability tend to be those who are relatively more risk averse and those who belong to groups that have a relatively good record for reliability. The possibility exists of an equilibrium involving self-confirming preconceptions in which groups that are not intrinsically different obtain good reputations for reliability with consistently different frequencies.

References

Azariadis, C.: Implicit contracts and under-employment equilibria. *Journal of Political Economy 83*, 1183–1202, December 1975.

Baily, M. N.: Wages and employment under uncertain demand. *Review of Economic Studies 41*, 37–50, January 1974.

Foley, D. K. & Hellwig, M. F.: Asset

management with trading uncertainty. *Review of Economic Studies 42*, 327–346, July 1975.

Freeman, S.: An economic model of academic early retirement. RCA Laboratories Technical Report, September 1975.

Gordon, D. F.: A neo-classical theory of Keynesian unemployment. *Economic Inquiry 12*, 431–459, December 1974.

Grossman, H. I.: The nature of optimal labor contracts. Read at Third Reisensburg Symposium, *On the stability of contemporary economic systems*, July 1975.

Grossman, H. I.: Adverse selection, dissembling, and competitive equilibrium. Unpublished manuscript, February 1977.

Grossman, H. I.: Risk shifting, layoffs, and seniority. Unpublished manuscript, June 1977.

Knight, F. H.: *Risk, uncertainty, and profit.* Houghton Mifflin, New York, 1921.

Riley, J. G.: Competitive signaling. *Journal of Economic Theory 10*, 174–186, April 1975.

Rothschild, M. & Stiglitz, J. E.: Equilibrium in competitive insurance markets: An essay on the economics of imperfect information. *Quarterly Journal of Economics 90*, 629–649, November 1976.

Salop, J. & Salop, S.: Self selection and turnover in the labor market. *Quarterly Journal of Economics 90*, 619–627, November 1976.

Shavell, S.: Sharing risks of deferred payment. *Journal of Political Economy 84*, 161–168, February 1976.

Spence, M.: Job market signaling. *Quarterly Journal of Economics 87*, 355–374, August 1973.

Stiglitz, J.: Incentives and risk sharing in sharecropping. *Review of Economic Studies 41*, 219–255, April 1974.

EXERCISES IN CONJECTURAL EQUILIBRIA

Frank H. Hahn

University of Cambridge, Cambridge, England

Abstract

In this paper one considers an economy in which individuals can transact at "false" prices. When they do they encounter quantity constraints, this in turn, as Arrow has noted, stops them acting as perfect competitors. In particular they must form an hypothesis concerning a possibility of affecting their quantity constraints by a change of price. This hypothesis is called a conjecture. A set of prices and quantity signals at which desired trades are achieved and no prices change is advantageous under the conjecture is a conjectural equilibrium. Economies can have conjectural equilibria even when they have a Walrasian one. Naturally one wants a theory of conjecture formation. In what follows it is shown, mainly by examples, that it is not fruitful to look for rational conjectural equilibria (defined in the sequel). One concludes that at best one could hope that agents conjecture Marshallian schedules.

I. Introduction

In orthodox theory an agent is described by his endowment, tastes and technological production possibilities which are open to him. One does not enquire how these characteristics of the agent came to be what they are, nor, in general, does one allow the characteristics to be affected by the economic environment. The characteristics are arbitrarily given by the history of the economy and of the agent and so, for instance, there are many equilibria depending on the characteristics. In particular if the total endowment of goods is given, *any allocation* of these between agents (in a pure exchange economy), will be an equilibrium for some tastes and endowment distribution. There does not seem to me anything wrong with the conclusion that equilibria are not history free (they are not independent of initial conditions). Indeed one may adduce rather strong arguments to support the view that history free theorems in the Social Sciences are bogus. To say that the equilibrium set depends on history is not to make equilibrium theory vacuous, the reverse is the case. For one is thereby taking the view that empirical evidence is required to generate interesting propositions. The relevance of these remarks to what follows will be seen below.

---

* This work was supported by National Science Foundation Grant SOC74-11446 at the Institute for Mathematical Studies in the Social Sciences, Stanford University.

The orthodox description of the agent is however incomplete on several counts. The most important omission concerns the information available to the agent. For instance if one considers the set of all physical objects in an economy a partition of this set will define the goods which one agent can distinguish. The partition may differ between agents and need not be independent of economic signals. One need only think of second-hand motor cars or different qualities of labour to see that an assumption that all agents have identical fine partitions is not satisfactory. *Pari passu* the same remarks apply to the partitioning of states of nature; see Radner (1968). A great deal of work has recently been undertaken mainly in the context of very simple models, to study the consequences of enriching the agent's description by endowing him with an information structure and taking account of the possibility that this structure may be only partly a characteristic, i.e. may in part at least depend on economic events (e.g. Rothschild, 1974).

Related to this is the observation that agents have, in general, to deduce their economic environment from the signals which they receive. Thus in orthodox theory the agent does not know the production possibility set of the economy but only relative prices. One of the beautiful aspects of the theory is that this is all he needs to know. Yet even in this simple orthodox world there is a theoretical lacuna: there is no description in terms of the decisions of agents of how prices come to be what they are. It is true that there is a very special account of exchange processes between agents which terminate in allocations which can be supported by competitive prices. But that is hardly satisfactory although even such special constructions may be superior to the auctioneer. For most markets it is simply the case that the description of the agent and of the signals which he receives is not rich enough for a theory of price formation by the agents. I have now come to the central issues to be studied in this paper. Since they are easy to misunderstand I shall discuss them further before introducing technicalities.

The proposal to study an economy which is sufficiently well described to answer the question: "why are the signals received by agents what they are?" is not at all to embark on "dynamics", except in a very weak sense. The weak sense is that an equilibrium must be recognizable as a stationary state of a dynamic system, the finer characteristics of which may be unknown. For instance, in the orthodox tâtonnement matters are normally too complicated to give a precise account of the evolution of prices from a given starting point. But the dynamic equations induce the definition of an equilibrium as stationary points. If the auctioneer is replaced by the agents who change the prices at which they are willing to trade whenever they consider this to be profitable then the stationary point of the dynamic system will have to be a set of signals at which agents do not see profits to be made by changing price. The set of stationary points or equilibria may include those of the tâtonnement but clearly need not coincide with the set of equilibria of the latter. I am making the obvious point that the states which we designate as equilibria cannot be independent of the theory of how signals and allocations change. The underlying axiom of the Arrow-Debreu theory is that (at positive prices), prices are stationary iff target excess demand is everywhere zero. If this assumption is changed, and nothing else in the description of the economy is changed, we may expect to find states which previously did not, and now do, qualify as equilibrium states.

At prices which are not in the stationary set of prices for a tâtonnement it is true by definition that not all agents can carry out their intended transactions. One postulates that this gives rise to a further set of signals which tell some of the agents that the transactions which are open to them at these prices are restricted in size. One now requires a theory or rule of the generation of such *quantity signals* (e.g. a "rationing scheme"), and one requires a theory of the agents' adjustments to these signals. It is in this second stage that one needs the notion of *conjectures*. If we include in the actions of an agent not only the amounts of each good which he wishes to trade but also the prices which he will announce as those at which he is willing to trade then in the first instance we are looking for a correspondence from the signals received by an agent to the set of actions he conjectures to be available to him. Call it the *action correspondence*. The equilibrium notion is fairly clear: it is signals received by agents such that the best action for each in the set of possible actions again induces the original signals. A formal definition is found below. Such an equilibrium I want to call a *conjectural equilibrium*.

I can now return to my opening paragraph. Certainly in the above description of a conjectural equilibrium the designated equilibrium states depend on the conjectures with which we have endowed the agents—e.g. their beliefs of the relation there might be between their ration and their announced price. But the conjectures are unexplained and to that extent conjectural equilibria appear to be arbitrary. As a first reply one is tempted to say that this is no different from the arbitrary tastes of orthodoxy. Certainly this is not entirely unjustified. But there is an objection to this, namely that it may be more convincing to believe that there is no clear inducement to discover which are "correct" tastes. I am not at all sure that this objection has much force. A person brought up on hamburgers may continue with this unpleasing diet even if it is the case that if he tried fish and chips he would discover that he preferred that. Just in the same way a person may continue to find himself unemployed ever so often at a given wage and conjecture wrongly that he can do nothing about it by proposing a lower wage and never undertake the experiment which would reveal this mistake. The belief of the orthodox that given sufficient time men discover their true environment suggests a certain ignorance of both anthropology and history. Children were sacrificed for good harvests for centuries and many people believe that the quantity of money determines the level of money income. Both are wrong conjectures.

That conjectures may be the outcome of past experience and that they may be "given" for the theorist and discoverable by empirical enquiry is to me acceptable. It is a view which decisively divides both Keynesians and Marxists from orthodoxy. The world is to be explained at least partly by the way agents perceive it and the way in which they perceive it is partly for history, partly for sociology, and partly for psychology. To the orthodox perception does not enter in the story. That is of course why they are so sanguine about the working of the invisible hand.

Nonetheless the orthodox pose an interesting problem when they suggest that the arbitrariness of conjectures be removed by the requirement that they be "correct". As we shall see that requirement is not unambiguously defined and may be impossible to satisfy. In what follows I shall be mainly concerned with that problem.

II. A Simple Conjectural Economy

Let there be H households, F firms and $(l+1)$ goods. The generic subscript of an agent is a and $a=h$ refers to a household and $a=i$ to a firm producing good i. Each firm produces only one good and each good is produced by a different firm. The subscript $i=0$ refers to leisure. The production sets $Y_i \subset R^{l+1}$ of all firms are strictly convex and $y_i \in Y_i$ is the vector with $y_{ii} \geq 0$, $y_{i0} \leq 0$ and $y_{ij}=0$, $j \neq i$, 0. Good i is produced by only the input of leisure. All Y_i are compact and $y_i \in Y_i$, $y_{ii} \neq 0 \to y_{i0} < 0$. Households have strictly convex closed preferences on R_+^{l+1}, are endowed with $l_{h0} > 0$ units of leisure (and nothing else) and receive the profit of firms which are distributed among them according to a fixed rule. One writes $x_h \in R^{l+1}$ as the demand vector of h, $x = \sum_n x_h$. Lastly let $\hat{y} \in X^I R^{l+1}$ be the allocation of production among firms.

I shall assume here that households have perfectly competitive conjectures. By this I mean that households choose x_h which is best in their preferences from the budget set.

$$B_h(p, \hat{y}) = \{x_h \mid px_h \leq p_0 l_{h0} + \Sigma \beta_{hi} p \cdot y_i\}$$

where $0 \leq \beta_{hi} \leq 1$ each i.

By my assumption this gives rise to the demand functions:

$$x_h = x_h(p, \hat{y}) \text{ all } h.$$

Let firm i observe the price vector $p \in R_+^{l+1}$, the demand x_i and a labour ration $L_{i0} < 0$. The latter is a signal that firm i must choose its production at p from $Y_i \cap \{y_i \mid y_{i0} \geq L_{i0}\}$. We stipulate

$$\sum_i L_{i0} = \sum_h (x_{h0} - l_{h0})$$

Now write

$$\pi_i(p, x_i, L_{i0}, y_i)$$

as the conjectured profit function of firm i. We postulate the following properties:

$\pi.1$ $\pi_i(p, x_i, L_{i0}, y_i) = p \cdot y$ for y_i with $y_{ii} = x_i$, $y_{i0} = L_{i0}$

$\pi.2$ $\pi_i(p, x_i, L_{i0}) < p \cdot y_i$ for $y_{ii} \geqslant x_i$, $y_{i0} \leqslant L_{i0}$ and at least one inequality strict.

$\pi.3$ $\pi_i(p, x_i, L_{i0}, y_i) > p \cdot y_i$ for $y_{ii} \leqslant x_i$, $y_{i0} \geqslant L_{i0}$ and at least one inequality strict.

$\pi.4$ Given (p, x_i, L_{i0}), π_i is concave in y_{ii} and $-y_{i0}$

Each firm i chooses $y_i \in Y_i$ given the signal (p, x_i, L_{i0}) to attain the highest conjectural profit. Notice that $\pi.2$ for instance implies that the firm conjectures that it must sell at a lower price than p_i if it wants to produce more than x_i and/or buy labour at a higher price than p_0 if it wants to employ more than L_{i0}. We may write the production choice of firm i as

$$y_i = y_i(p, x_i, L_{i0}).$$

Lastly write $L_0 = \{L_{10} \dots L_{H0}\}$.

D.2.1. We say that $p^0, L_0^0, (x_1^0 \dots x_H^0), \hat{y}^0$ is a *conjectural equilibrium* if

(a) $x_h^0 \geqslant_h x_h$ all $x_h \in B_h(p^0, \hat{y}^0)$ all h

(b) $p^0 y_i^0 = \pi_i(p^0, x_i^0, L_{i0}^0, y_i^0) \geqslant \pi_i(p^0, x_i^0, L_{i0}, y_i)$ all $y_i \in Y_i$ all i

(c) $y_{ii}^0 = x_i^0$ all $i = 1 \dots l$

(d) $\sum y_{i0}^0 = \sum L_{i0}^0$ when $\sum_i L_{i0}^0 = \sum_h (x_{h0}^0 - l_{h0})$

The definition is straightforward. Of course the economy considered is somewhat special in particular in insisting that households are endowed with competitive conjectures. In the sequel I shall follow tradition and not ask that these conjectures of households correspond to what is the case.

Now the profit functions $\pi_i(\cdot)$ embody the conjectures of firms and at the moment are arbitrary up to $\pi.1-\pi.4$. In studying the notion of rational conjectures it will be as well not to be too ambitious at the outset. In particular I shall start with considering the possibility of imposing *local* restrictions on conjectures.

To do this I need to define a conjectural equilibrium relatively to the production of firm i. Let $p^0, L_0^0, (x_1^0 \dots x_H^0), \hat{y}^0$ be a conjectural equilibrium and consider $y_i \in N(\varepsilon, y_i^0)$ where $N(\cdot)$ is a small, (ε), neighbourhood of y_i^0 in R^{l+1}. Then

D.2.2. Let $p(y_i)$, $L_0(y_i)$, $(x_1(y_i) \ldots x_H(y_i))$, $\hat{y}(y_i)$ be called[1] a *conjectural equilibrium relatively to* $y_i \in N(\varepsilon, y_i^0)$ if

a) $x_h(y_i) \geqslant_h x_h$ all $x_h \in B_h(p(y_i), \hat{y}(y_i))\}$ all h

b) $p(y_i) y_k(y_i) = \pi_k(p(y_i), \ x_k(y_i),' \ L_{k0}(y_i), \ y_k(y_i)) \geqslant \pi_k(p(y_i), \ x_k(y_i), \ L_{k0}(y_i), \ y_k)$ all $y_k \in Y_k$ *and* all $k \neq i$.

c) $y_{kk}(y_i) = x_k(y_i)$ all $k = 1 \ldots l$

(d) $\sum_k y_{k0}(y_i) = \sum_k L_{k0}(y_i)$ and $\sum_k L_{k0}(y_i) = \sum_h (x_{h0}(y_i) - l_{k0})$

It will be seen that the difference between a conjectural equilibrium and a conjectural equilibrium relatively to y_i is that in the former we do, and in the latter we do not, demand that firm i should have maximum profits under its conjectures. The reason for this construction will become clear almost at one.

Let $E_i(y_i, y_i^0, \varepsilon) \subset R^{l+1} \times R^H \times R_+^{H(l+1)} \times R^{(F \cdot 1)(l+1)}$ be the set of conjectural equilibria relative to y_i when $y_i \in N(y_i^0, \varepsilon)$. An element of $E_i(\cdot)$ is $(p(y_i), L(y_i), (x_1(y_1) \ldots x_H(y_i), \hat{y}(y_i))$. I write $E_{ip}(\cdot)$ as the projection of $E_i(\cdot)$ onto the price space.

D.2.3. I call $(p^0, x_1^0 \ldots x_H^0, L_0^0, y^0)$ an ε-*reasonable* conjectural equilibrium if for all $i = 1 \ldots e$ and given ε

either a) $p_i y_i \leqslant \pi_i(p^0, x_i^0 L_{i0}^0, y_i^0)$, $p_i \in E_{ip}(y_i, y_i^0, \varepsilon)$, $y_i \in Y_i \cap N(g_i^0, \varepsilon)$

or b) $E_i(y_i, y_i^0, \varepsilon)$ is empty.

Let me explain the idea of D.2.3. One considers a given conjectural equilibrium and asks what would happen to the equilibrium profits of a firm i if it deviated slightly in its production plan from what, under its conjectures is an optimum plan. If such a slight deviation is inconsistent, given the conjectures of *all other firms* with an equilibrium (D.2.3.b), we argue that it is reasonable for firm i not to undertake that deviation. If it is consistent with such an equilibrium but profits are no higher for firm i than they were without that deviation (D.2.3.a) we also argue that the firm i is reasonable in not making the deviation. In this of course D.2.3.b is the least attractive. But unless one is willing to open the Pandora's box of dynamics there is not much alternative.

I use the terminology 'reasonable' to distinguish the case where a firm may be right in its belief that it cannot locally improve profits for the 'wrong' reason from that where the firm is right in that belief for the 'right' reason (which I shall call 'rational'). Thus a firm may wrongly predict the relevant elements of $E_i(\cdot)$ and yet be correct in its conclusion that it cannot improve itself by small changes in production. A more stringent requirement is that in a conjectural equilibrium each firm i should correctly predict the element of $E_i(\cdot)$. Thus

---

[1] The ith vector of $\hat{y}(y_i)$ is y_i.

D.2.4. I call $(p^0, x_1^0 \ldots x_H^0, L^0, \hat{y}^0)$ an *ε-rational* conjectural equilibrium if

a) If is an ε-reasonable equilibrium

and b) For all i and $y_i \in Y_i \cap N(\varepsilon, y_i^0)$

$$p_i y_i = \pi_i(p, x_i, L_{i0}, y) \quad \text{where} \quad (p, x_1, \ldots, x_H, L_0, \hat{y}) \in E_i(y_i, y_i^0).$$

Thus in an ε-rational conjectural equilibrium not only is there no other conjectural equilibrium consistent with $y_i \in N(y_i^0, \varepsilon)$ in which i's profits are higher than they are in the given equilibrium, but the profits attained in any conjectural equilibrium relatively to y_i are those which i's conjectures predict.

Both of the definitions of ε-reasonable and ε-rational conjectural equilibrium are in the general equilibrium spirit and it may be thought that they are too demanding even before one has considered the problem of their existence. So let me consider one last alternative formulation which is more in the spirit of Nash equilibria.

Let $\hat{y}_N^0(y_i)$ be the vector $\hat{y}^0$ with y_i replacing y_i^0. (The subscript N reminds us of the Nash feature that the production vectors of firms other than i are fixed.) We require the notion of an ε-Nash deviation from a conjectural equilibrium relatively to y_i

D.2.5. Let $(p^0, x_1^0, \ldots, x_H^0, L_0^0, \hat{y}^0)$ be a conjectural equilibrium. Then $p^N(y_i) \in R_+^{l+1}$, $x_h^N(y_i) \in R_+^{l+1}$, $(h = 1, \ldots, H)$, $L_0^N(y_i) \in R^H$ is called an *ε-Nash deviation* from the given conjectural equilibrium relatively y_i if when $y_i \in Y_i N(\varepsilon, y_i^0)$:

(a) $x_h^N(y_i) \geqslant_h x_h$ all $x_h \in B_h(p^N(y_i), \hat{y}_N^0(y_i))$ all h

(b) $\sum_h x_{hk}^N(y_i) = y_{kk}^0$ all $k \neq i$

$\sum_h x_{hi}^N(y_i) = y_{ii}$

$\sum_h (x_{h0}^N(y_i) - l_{h0}) = \sum L_{0k}^N(y_i) = \sum_{k \neq i} y_{k0}^0 + y_{i0}$

Thus in an ε-Nash deviation we calculate the equilibrium of the economy on the supposition that all firms other than i keep their productions as it is in conjectural equilibrium and therefore ignore the fact that this constancy of production may not be profit maximising for these firms under their conjectures. One may say that this is an interesting concept either because no firm i could calculate anything more elaborate or, more speculatively that for a small enough firm i at ε, the ε-Nash deviation is a good approximation to an ε-conjectural equilibrium relatively to y_i. One now has

D.2.6. The conjectural equilibrium $(p^0, x_1, \ldots, x_H^0 L_0^0, \hat{y}^0)$ is *ε-Nash rational* if for all i and $y_i \in Y_i \cap N(\varepsilon, y_i)$ there exists an ε-Nash deviation relatively to i such that

$$p^N(y_i) y_i = \pi_i(p^N(y_i), x_i^N(y_i), L_{0i}^N(y_i), y_i)$$

That is, in an ε-Nash rational conjectural equilibrium the conjectural profit functions of firms correctly predict the profits to be made from an ε-Nash deviation.

We now have a good many candidates for tying down conjectures. One wants to ask two questions: (i) are there good economic grounds for supposing conjectural equilibria to have one or more of the characteristics captured by ε-reasonable, ε-rational and ε-Nash rational? and (ii) are all of these equilibria non-vacuous—that is, could they exist? Until we have explored (ii) it is not worthwhile arguing about (i).

III. Existence Problems

Given the assumptions in Section II one can show that a conjectural equilibrium exists[1] and I shall here take this for granted. To proceed to the next task it will be convenient to simplify the model in the non-essential way of letting firms have competitive conjectures in the labour market. That is we now remove the quantity signals L_{i0} from the profit functions. I shall also suppose that a conjectural equilibrium with $p_0 > 0$ exists and henceforth, without change of notation, take $p_0 = 1$ in p. Lastly I postulate that all functions that interest me are of class C^2.

Let $\hat{\pi} = (\pi_1, ..., \pi_\iota)$ be the vector of profits $p \cdot y_i$. Let us also now write

$$y_{i0} = f_i(y_{ii}) \qquad\qquad 3.1$$

for the input of labour required to produce y_{ii}. One takes $f_i(\cdot)$ as convex. From what has already been said one may write

$$x_i = x_i(p, \hat{y})$$

and so

$$x_i - y_{ii} \equiv g_i(p, \hat{y})$$

where without change of notation I now take $\hat{y} \in R_+^l$ to be the vector of outputs. Also if $\pi_i(p_i, x_i, y_{ii})$ is the conjectural profit function, let

$$h_i(p_i, x_i, y_{ii}) \equiv \bar{h}_i(p, \hat{y}) \equiv \frac{\partial \pi_i}{\partial y_{ii}}$$

Then $(p^0, \hat{y}^0)$ is a conjectural equilibrium if

$$
\left.
\begin{array}{l}
\text{a)} \ \ g(p^0, y^0) = 0 \\
\text{b)} \ \ \bar{h}(p^0, y^0) = 0
\end{array}
\right\} \qquad\qquad 3.1
$$

---

[1] A proof for closely related models will be found in Hahn (forthcoming) and Negishi (1968).

Suppose that $(p^0, \hat{y}^0) \gg 0$ and let the superscript 0 to a function denote that it is evaluated at $(p^0, \hat{y}^0)$. Then the conjectural equilibrium is called *regular* if

$$M(p^0, \hat{y}^0) = \begin{bmatrix} g_p^0 & g_y^0 \\ \bar{h}_p^0 & \bar{h}_y^0 \end{bmatrix}$$

is of full rank (i.e. of rank $2l$).

It will be convenient to state the regularity condition in a different form. Let H always denote an $l \times l$ diagonal matrix where

$$H_p^0 = [h_{ip_i}^0], \ H_x^0 = [h_{ix_i}^0], \ H_y^0 = [h_{iy_{ii}}^0], \ H_z^0 = h_{ix_i}^0 + h_{iy_{ii}}^0]$$

Then

$$\bar{h}_p^0 = H_p^0 + H_x^0 x_p = H_p^0 + H_x^0 g_p^0$$

$$\bar{h}_y^0 = H_y^0 + H_x^0 x_y = H_y^0 + H_x^0 + H_x^0 [x_y - I] = H_y^0 + H_x^0 + H_x^0 g_y^0$$

Hence if $M(p^0, \hat{y}^0)$ is non-singular so is $M^*(p^0, \hat{y}^0)$ where

$$M^*(p^0, \hat{y}^0) = \begin{bmatrix} g_p^0 & g_y^0 \\ H_p^0 & H_z^0 \end{bmatrix}$$

D.3.1. A conjectural equilibrium $(p^0, \hat{y}^0)$ will be called *regular* if $(p^0, \hat{y}^0) \gg 0$ and $M^*(p^0, \hat{y}^0)$ is of full rank.

Now consider a regular conjectural equilibrium and take a small variation in the production of firm k. We want to find the conjectural equilibrium (if it exists), relatively to $(y_{kk}^0 \pm \varepsilon)$ where ε is very small. Suppose this conjectural equilibrium is $(p, \hat{y})$. Then it must satisfy:

$$\left. \begin{aligned} g_p^0(p - p^0) + g_y^0(\hat{y} - \hat{y}^0) &= 0 \\ \text{and } \bar{h}_{ip}^0(p - p^0) + \bar{h}_{iy}^0(\hat{y} - \hat{y}^0) &= 0 \quad \text{all } i = k \end{aligned} \right\} \qquad 3.2$$

Also one has $y_{kk}^0(p_k - p_k^0) + (p_k^0 + f_k'(y_{kk}^0))(y_{kk} - y_{kk}^0) = \pi_k - \pi_k^0$ $\qquad 3.3$

So if $H_p^0(k)$ is the matrix H_p^0 with its kth diagonal element replaced by y_{kk}^0 and $H_z^0(k)$ is the matrix H_z^0 with its kth diagonal element replaced by $(p_k^0 + f_k'(y_k^0 k))$ one is interested in the equations

$$M_k^*(p^0, y^0)(p - p^0, y - y^0) = \{\delta_{ik+l}(\pi_k - \pi_k^0)\} \qquad 3.4$$

where

$$M_k^*(p^0, \hat{y}^0) = \begin{bmatrix} g_p^0 & g_y^0 \\ H_p^0(k) & H_z^0(k) \end{bmatrix}$$

Proposition 3.1. A necessary and sufficient condition for a regular conjectural equilibrium to be ε-rational for ε arbitrarily small is that *either* the matrix

$M_K^*(p^0, \hat{y}^0)$ be singular for all $k=1, ..., l$ *or* that no equilibria relatively to $(y_{kk}^0 \pm \varepsilon)$ exist for any[1] k.

Proof. (a) *Necessity.* If $(p^0, \hat{y}^0)$ is a conjectural equilibrium and $M_k^*(p^0, \hat{y}^0)$ is of full rank for some k then 3.4 has a solution with $\pi_k > \pi_k^0$ so that the equilibrium would not be ε-reasonable and so not ε-rational.

(b) *Sufficiency.* If at $(p^0, \hat{y}^0)$ the condition of the proposition is satisfied then one can solve

$$M_k^*(p^0, \hat{y}^0)(p - p^0, \hat{y} - \hat{y}^0) = \{0\}$$

for all the conjectural equilibria $(p, \hat{y})$ relatively to $(y_{kk}^b \pm \varepsilon)$. In all such equilibria $\pi_k = \pi_k^0$ and there exists no such equilibrium with $\pi_k > \pi_k^0$.

The proposition is of course trivial—indeed it is almost a definition of an ε-rational conjectural equilibrium. Nonetheless it is of some help with the rather intractable problem of whether ε-rational equilibria exist. To see this I consider an example.

Suppose that the conjectural profit function of each firm is derived from the conjectural inverse demand function:

$$p_i + \beta_i(y_{ii} - x_i). \quad \beta_i < 0 \text{ all } i \qquad 3.5$$

Also assume that

$$f_i(y_{ii}) = -c_i y_{ii} \quad c_i > 0 \text{ all } i \qquad 3.6$$

Then one verifies that $H_p^0 = I$, $H_z^0 = \{\beta_i\}$ while $H_p^0(k)$ has y_{kk}^0 in the kth diagonal place and $H_z^0(k)$ has $-\beta_k y_{kk}^0$ as the kth diagonal element.

Let us consider only regular conjectural equilibria for this economy so that writing small letters for the determinant of the matrix, $m^*(p, \hat{y}) \neq 0$ at any conjectural equilibrium $(p, \hat{y})$. In the present economy one has

$$m_{l+k, k}^* + \beta_k m_{l+k, l+k}^* = m^*$$

where I now omit the arguments $(p, \hat{y})$ and where m_{ij}^* are co-factors in the usual notation. If the conjectural equilibrium is ε-rational and we use Proposition 3.1 in the present case one must have

$$m_{l+k, k}^* - \beta_k m_{l+k, l+k}^* = 0$$

and since this must hold for all k one now has

$$m_{l+k, k}^* = \tfrac{1}{2} m^* \quad \text{all } k \qquad 3.7$$

Now let us specialise somewhat further by assuming (i) $l = 2$. (ii) all households have parallel linear Engel curves and (iii) labour is supplied inelastically and leisure does not enter the utility function.

---

[1] I shall henceforth in this section ignore the second contingency. Throughout I am strictly concerned with "infinitesimal rationality", i.e. with $\varepsilon \to 0$. But the exposition will serve if sufficient regularity is granted.

It is a consequence of (ii) that g_p becomes a matrix of substitution terms which in view of (iii) is singular. Also a typical element of g_y is $x_{iy_i} - \delta_{ij}$. If μ is the sum of profits and wages then

$$x_{iy_i} = x_{i\mu}(p_j - c_j) = -\beta_j x_{i\mu} y_{jj}$$

by (iii) where $x_{i\mu} = \partial x_i / \partial \mu$. Also by (iii) $\Sigma p_i x_{i\mu} = 1$. Using all of this and 3.7 one finds that we require of a regular conjectural equilibrium that[1]

(A) $c_1 \beta_2 S_{12} + c_2 \beta_1 s_1 = 0$

where S_{ij} is a substitution term. From this and (iii) one has

$$\frac{c_1 \beta_2}{p_2} = \frac{c_2 \beta_1}{p_1^0} = k \qquad\qquad 3.8$$

We also require

(B) $x_{1\mu}[\beta_1 c_2 x_1 - \beta_2 c_1 x_2] + c_2 = 0$

or using 3.8

$$kx_1 \mu[p_1^0 x_1 - p_2^0 x_2] + c_2 = 0 \qquad\qquad 3.9$$

These two conditions must be satisfied if the conjectural equilibrium is to be ε-rational. But now suppose the common utility function to be Cobb-Douglas with exponents α_i $(i = 1, 2)$. Then 3.9 becomes

$$k\mu x_{i\mu}[\alpha_1 - \alpha_2] + c_2 = 0 \qquad\qquad 3.9'$$

Since one wants $k < 0$ it now follows that should $\alpha_2 > \alpha_1$ no ε-rational regular conjectural equilibrium exists.

As a second example consider profit conjectures based on the following conjectural inverse demand functions:

$$p_i(y_{ii}/x_i)^{\beta_i} \text{ where } -1 < \beta_i < 0 \qquad\qquad 3.10$$

Then one verifies that $H_p^0 = \{1 + \beta_i\}$, $H_z^0 = \{0\}$, $H_p^0(k)$ has y_{kk}^0 in the kth diagonal place and H_z^0 has $-\beta_k p_k^0$. We now assume that $c_1 = c_2 = c$ and continue the assumptions (i) to (iii) of the previous example.

The rather tedious manipulations will be found in the appendix. Using Proposition 3.1 one shows that if a given conjectural equilibrium is to be ε-rational one requires

$$-\frac{\sigma_{21}}{\sigma_{11}} = \frac{\beta_1(1 + \beta_2)}{\beta_2(1 + \beta_1)} \qquad\qquad 3.11$$

---

[1] See Appendix for manipulations.

and also that

$$-\frac{\sigma_{21}}{\sigma_{11}} > 1 \qquad\qquad 3.12$$

where σ_{ij} is the compensated elasticity of demand for good i for a change in the price of good j. From elementary theory then 3.12 can also be written as

$$\frac{x_1^0}{x_2^0} > 1 \qquad\qquad 3.13$$

From 3.11 also $|\beta_1| > |\beta_2|$ and so since $p_i^0(1+\beta_i) = ci = 1,\ 2$ one has

$$p_1^0 > p_2^0 \qquad\qquad 3.14$$

But now it is easy to find a hypothesis which makes the fulfilment of these conditions impossible. For instance let the common strictly quasiconcave function be homothetic with the indifference curves having a unitary slope where they cross the 45° line. Then 3.13 and 3.14 together are not possible.

If one has enough patience one can construct other 'well behaved' economies which have no regular ε-rational conjectural equilibrium. Thus one can relatively easily find examples with three goods where the requirements of Proposition 3.1 conflict with the concavity of the conjectured profit function.

The examples suggest that there will be considerable difficulty in describing an economy with simple enough conjectures which also possesses an ε-rational equilibrium. My present view is that the conditions will turn out to be sufficiently restrictive to make the result uninteresting. But there is another lesson which seems important.

In the examples I gave conjectures a particular form. Now if one takes ε small enough what one is roughly concerned with is the existence of an equilibrium where the conjectured slope of the inverse demand curve at the equilibrium output accurately predicts the price in an equilibrium relatively to a very small deviation in a producer's output. But as we have seen this will depend not only on the conjectured slopes of other producers but also on their rates of change (the terms h_p, h_y). In the examples, in trying to discover whether conjectured slopes can be 'tied down' by asking that they be 'correct' in a proper sense we made these higher order terms *arbitrary*. So even had our conclusion been positive we should have shown that there exists an equilibrium in which conjectured slopes are 'correct' only at the cost of arbitrarily imposing a form on the conjectured demand function. Indeed I think that under fairly general assumptions one may be able to show that there always exists a conjectural equilibrium with "correct" slopes provided one can arbitrarily specify the form of the conjecture. But this means that we do not escape the arbitrariness of conjectures.

Evidently there are quite hard technical problems and they require further investigation. But I think there is enough evidence in this section to warrant the preliminary conclusion that ε-rationality is not a hopeful way of avoiding the arbitrariness—i.e. the exogenous, nature of conjectures.

IV. Nash ε-Rationality

I shall be brief in this section for the matter requires more investigation than I can give it here. Indeed I shall only consider an example of $l=2$.

Suppose that $(p^0, \hat{y}^0)$ is a conjectural equilibrium and consider a small ε deviation from y_{11}^0 by producer one. We are in the first instance interested in the equilibria (if they exist), relatively to that deviation on the supposition that the output of producer two stays at y_{22}^0. Notice that such equilibria will not in general be conjectural equilibria since producer two will not be maximising relatively to his conjectures. Now p will be an equilibrium relatively to $(y_{11}^0 \pm \varepsilon)$ when ε is small enough if it satisfies

$$g_p^0(p - p^0) = - g_{y_1}^0(y_{11} - y_{11}^0)$$

where g_p^0 has the usual meaning and $g_{y_1}^0 \in R^2$ is the vector $(x_{1y_1} - 1, x_{2y_1})$.

This equation can be solved, when $(y_{11} - y_{11}^0) \neq 0$ iff g_p^0 is not singular. But in one of our examples where households supply labour inelastically and where they ave parallel linear Engel curves, g_p^0 is a singular matrix of substitution terms. Let us call an economy where households satisfy these assumptions Hicksian (cf. Arrow & Hahn, 1971). Then

Proposition 4.1. Any conjectural equilibrium of a Hicksian economy where labour is supplied inelastically is ε-Nash rational for ε small enough.

This result is a direct consequence of our general decision to call conjectures rational if deviations in the actions of one agent are not compatible with equilibrium (D.2.3.b). Of course, this is open to argument. Yet it is not easy to see what alternative route should be followed in this case. One could, for instance, relax the purely Walrasian equilibrium notion (and consider equilibria with rationing) or one could try to model the 'true' dynamics of the economy which would give an answer to the agent's question: what will be the case if I deviate slightly from my present actions? But not only is this procedure technically and conceptually hard; it is one which makes it even more impossible to suppose that agents can carry out correct calculations.

So let me now suppose that g_p^0 is not singular which I achieve in the Hicksian economy by dropping the assumption that labour is inelastically supplied (i.e. that it does not enter the utility function). Let

$$N_1^0 = \begin{bmatrix} g_p^0 & g_{y_1}^0 \\ y_{11}^0 & p_1^0 - c_1 \end{bmatrix}$$

Then if the conjectural equilibrium is ε-Nash rational one wants N_1^0 to be singular. The argument here is exactly as in the previous section the only difference being that $y_{22} = y_{22}^0$ by construction.

To see the difficulties one may now encounter let the common utility function be Cobb-Douglas with exponents α_i $(i = 0 \ldots 2)$ where the subscript 0 refers to leisure. Suppose further that conjectures have the form of 3.9, and choose units so that $c_i = 1$, $i = 1, 2$.

Then the condition that N_1^0 be singular reduces in this special case to

$$\alpha_0 + \alpha_1 \alpha_2 - (1 - \alpha_2)\alpha_1 = \frac{1 + \beta_1}{\beta_1} \frac{(\alpha_2 - 1)}{\alpha_1}$$

For $\pi.1 - \pi.4$ to hold one wants β, < 0 and hence

$$\frac{\alpha_0}{1 - 2\alpha_2} > \alpha_0$$

If 4.1 is violated then no ε-Nash rational conjectural equilibrium is possible. For with $\beta_1 > 0$ no profit maximising choice of the firm exists while for $\beta_1 < 0$, N_1^0 cannot vanish.

Once again it is rather doubtful that one can find sufficiently general conditions which would ensure the existence of an ε-Nash rational conjectural equilibrium. But this is a matter for further study.

V. Some Conclusions

To a practical economist it will be no surprise that the notions of rationality in conjectures explored here are very unpromising. Indeed he would argue that the questions are incorrectly formulated. For either the typical firm is 'small' and hence one should ignore the general equilibrium repercussions of its own actions or it is significant in which case the proper approach is either game theoretic or a rule of thumb.

There evidently is some force in this objection. On the other hand unless a firm is so small (strictly of measure zero), as to make a perfectly competitive conjecture ε-rational in my sense, it will make mistakes when it acts on a conjectured demand curve derived from partial equilibrium hypotheses. By this I mean that it correctly calculates the slope of the demand curve on the hypothesis that all other prices and outputs other than its own are fixed. The question of course is whether these mistakes are small enough to be 'sensibly' ignored.

With sufficient assumptions (which certainly must exclude the Cobb-Douglas utility function) one can almost certainly establish the existence of a "Marshallian ε-conjectural equilibrium". That would be an equilibrium in which producers have chosen optimally relatively to observed demand and price and have correctly calculated the slope of their demand curve at this point on the assumption that all other prices and outputs remain constant. There will be some technical difficulties since one will not be sure without special hypotheses that conjectural profit functions are concave everywhere. But there certainly is a class of utility for which this will be true. Such equilibria will not be ε-reasonable or ε-rational. Hence in an actual experiment a firm may discover that it is mistaken. Depending on cross-elasticities these mistakes may be 'large' for a 'small' firm.

All of this requires further study and the present paper is no more than an introduction to some of the questions which arise. My present view is that if it will prove possible to make conjectures less arbitrary it will have to be done in a Marshallian way. This is not a conclusion congenial to a general equilibrium man.

Appendix

Linear Conjectures

$$m^* = \begin{vmatrix} S_{11} & S_{12} & x_{1\mu}(p_1-c_1)-1 & x_{1\mu}(p_2-c_2) \\ S_{21} & S_{22} & x_{2\mu}(p_1-c_1) & x_{2\mu}(p_2-c_2)-1 \\ 1 & 0 & \beta_1 & 0 \\ 0 & 1 & 0 & \beta_2 \end{vmatrix}$$

Adding p_1 times first row to p_2 times second row gives

$$m^* = \begin{vmatrix} S_{11} & S_{12} & x_{1\mu}(p_1-c_1)-1 & x_{1\mu}(p_2-c_2) \\ 0 & 0 & -c_1 & -c_2 \\ 1 & 0 & \beta_1 & 0 \\ 0 & 1 & 0 & \beta_a \end{vmatrix}$$

Let Δ be the top right-hand 2×2 determinant. Then

$$m^* = S_{11}\beta_1 c_2 - S_{12}\beta_2 c_1 + \Delta$$
$$m_{31}^* = -S_{12}c_1\beta_2 + \Delta$$
$$m_{41}^* = S_{11}c_2\beta_1 + \Delta$$

From 3.7: $m_{31}^* = m_{41}^*$ gives

$$S_{11}c_1\beta_1 + S_{12}c_1\beta_2 = 0$$

which is A of the text. For 3.7 also $2m_{31}^* = m^*$ or

$$S_{11}\beta_1 c_2 + S_{12}\beta_2 c_1 - \Delta = 0$$

and so

$$\Delta = c_2 - c_2 x_{1\mu}(p_1 - c_1) + c_1 x_{1\mu}(p_2 - c_2) = c_2 + [c_2\beta_1 x_1 - c_1\beta_2 x_2] = 0$$

which is B of the text.

Constant Elasticity Conjectures

We have

$$M^* = \begin{bmatrix} g_p^0 & g_y^0 \\ \{1+\beta_i\} & 0 \end{bmatrix}$$

whence

$$m^* = \prod^i (1+\beta_i)|g_y^0|$$

Proceeding as in the previous example and using $p_k^0 - c = -\beta_k p_k^0$ one finds

$$|g_y^0| = x_{1\mu}\beta_1 c p_1^0 - \beta_2 c p_2^0 + c \tag{A.1}$$

Also

$$\begin{bmatrix} g_{p_1}^0 & g_{p_2}^0 & g_{y_1}^0 & g_{y_2}^0 \\ y_{11}^0 & 0 & -\alpha_1 p_1^0 & 0 \\ 0 & (1+\beta_2) & 0 & 0 \end{bmatrix}$$

and similarly for M_2^*. One finds

$$m_1^* = (1+\beta_2)[x_1^0|g_y^0| - \beta_1 p_1^0 m_{33}^*]$$
$$m_2^* = (1+\beta_1)[x_2^0|g_y^0| - \beta_2 p_2^0 m_{44}^*]$$

Calculating further yields

$$m_{33}^* = -S_{11}(1+\beta_2)c, \quad m_{44}^* = S_{12}(1+\beta_1)c \tag{A.2}$$

By Proposition 3.1 one wants $m_1^* = m_2^* = 0$ if the equilibrium is to be ε-rational. So

$$\beta_1 p_1^0 m_{33}^*/x_1^0 = \beta_2 p_2^0 m_{44}^*/x_2^0 \tag{A.3}$$

or by (A.2)

$$-\beta_1(1+\beta_2)c\sigma_{11} = \beta_2(1+\beta_1)c\sigma_{12} \tag{A.4}$$

which then yields 3.11 of the text.

Next since $m_{33}^* > 0$, $m_{44}^* > 0$, $\beta_i > 0$ one must have

$$|g_y^0| < 0.$$

So from (A.1)

$$\frac{\beta_1 p_1^0}{\beta_2 p_2^0} = \frac{\beta_1(1+\beta_2)}{\beta_2(1+\beta_1)} > 1 \tag{A.5}$$

This confirms 3.12 of the text.

References

Arrow, K. J. & Hahn, F. H.: *General competitive analysis*. Holden Day, 1971.

Hahn, F. H.: On non-Walrasian equilibria. *Review of Economic Studies* (forthcoming).

Negishi, Y.: Monopolistic competition and general equilibrium. *Review of Economic Studies*, 1968.

Radner, R.: Competitive equilibrium under uncertainty. *Econometrica*, 1968.

Rothschild, M.: A two-armed-bandit theory of market pricing. *Journal of Economic Theory*, 1974.

WAGES AND THE DEMAND FOR LABOR IN UNEMPLOYMENT EQUILIBRIA*

Paavo Peisa

University of Helsinki, Helsinki, Finland

Abstract

This paper analyzes the demand for labor under conditions of Keynesian under-employment, where firms cannot sell as much as they wish at given market prices due to a lack of effective demand for output. It is argued that if the inventory holding motive is operative, labor will be demanded until the value of its marginal product is equal to the wage rate. Thus a *ceteris paribus* reduction in wages leads to a decrease in unemployment, contrary to the conclusion of the Barro–Grossman model.

I. Introduction

Barro & Grossman (1971) make a sharp distinction between price and quantity equilibrium situations. In price equilibrium, labor is demanded up to the point where the market value of output produced by the marginal worker is equal to the wage rate; consequently, quantity signals have no effect on labor demand. This is to be contrasted with quantity equilibrium, in which realized sales of output determine the demand for labor and changes in wages can only indirectly affect the level of employment by influencing the (effective) demand for output. A similar contrast appears in other fields of macroeconomic analysis, for example in liquidity and wealth explanations for consumption and saving, or credit availability and interest rate explanations for the transmission of monetary policy.

In the Barro–Grossman model, realized sales perform a double function. They constitute a proxy for expected future sales as well as a constraint on the current level of output.[1] In this paper, the role of inventories is examined in the context of the simple Barro–Grossman model. Attention is focused on the second aspect of realized sales, and the effects of changes in current variables on sales (as well as other) expectations are ignored.

---

* I wish to thank Professors J. Paunio and H. Grossman for useful comments on an earlier version of this paper, as well as Mr G. Bingham for his review.
[1] When considering the income–consumption relation (apparently with specific reference to the same Barro–Grossman model) Leijonhufvud (1973, p. 37) identified even a third aspect of realized sales, namely sales as a constraint on the demand signals currently emitted.

The conclusions which emerge are:

(i) if firms can store their output, the (effective) demand for labor inputs depends directly on the wage rate, so that a wage cut which does not reduce effective demand for output reduces unemployment; and

(ii) whenever the firm has positive inventories, its demand for labor is determined by the condition that the value of the marginal product of labor is equal to the wage rate, even if the sales constraint is effective; however, an increase in demand for output increases the demand for labor.

II. The Polar Cases

This analysis is limited to the demand for labor of a single firm only. It is assumed that the firm produces only one kind of putput and that labor is the only variable factor of production. The amount produced is given by $f(L)$ when the amount of labor employed is L; the production function $f(\cdot)$ has continuous derivatives $f'(\cdot) > 0$ and $f''(\cdot) < 0$ and, moreover, $f'(L) \to \infty$ as $L \to 0$. The product of the firm is taken as the *numéraire* and the (real) wage rate is denoted by w. In the subsequent discussion, it is assumed that the firm takes prices as given and that it can hire any amount of labor it wishes at the given wage rate.

The price vs. quantity equilibrium distinction can briefly be explained as follows.

In price equilibrium, the firm can sell as much of its output as it wants at the given price 1. The profit $f(L) - wL$ is maximized, when the amount of labor employed, L^*, satisfies the condition $w = f'(L^*)$. The boundary case $L^* = 0$ is excluded by the assumption that $f'(L) \to \infty$ as $L \to 0$. Diminishing returns to labor imply that the demand for labor is higher, the lower the wage rate; formally,

$$\frac{dL^*}{dw} = \frac{1}{f''(L^*)} < 0. \tag{1}$$

In quantity equilibrium, sales are restricted by the state of effective demand and the firm has to take the sales constraint into account when formulating its employment policy. If the upper bound for sales is denoted by Y, an additional constraint in the profit maximization problem is $Y \geq f(L)$. If w is small enough, the sales constraint is operative and the demand for labor is determined by the condition $Y = f(L^*)$. The demand for labor increases as the maximum amount of sales increases; formally

$$\frac{dL^*}{dY} = \frac{1}{f'(L^*)} > 0. \tag{2}$$

From a narrow point of view, we can say that the cause of unemployment is weak demand for labor. The interesting feature of eqs. (1) and (2) is that each relates the labor demand to only one variable. These two equations offer two distinct theories of the cause of unemployment.

The production function $f(\cdot)$ is best considered as a purely technological relationship between inputs and outputs. Although changes in it are not inconceivable, these, as well as the precise properties of $f(\cdot)$, do not have to be explained by the economic theorist; rather, the properties of $f(\cdot)$ can be taken as given. Therefore, we can say that in price equilibrium, an excessive wage rate is the cause of unemployment, whereas in quantity equilibrium the cause is a lack of demand. In quantity equilibrium, a change in effective demand is fully reflected by a change in output, but in price equilibrium it has no effect on employment, unless it induces a change in the real wage rate. A wage cut improves employment, which is determined by marginal condition (1), but in quantity equilibrium (2) the effect runs entirely through the indirect route, namely via effective demand Y and can obviously work in either direction. In quantity equilibrium, the marginal worker brings profit to the firm, and the volume of output could be profitably expanded at the existing wage rate only if there was a demand for the extra output; thus a reduction in wages does not directly give rise to a demand for labor.

The doctrinal history of the distinction between price and quantity equilibrium can readily be traced—through Patinkin—back to Keynes, and Keynesian analysis is commonly characterized as "quantity equilibrium analysis". However, Keynes accepted one of the two classical postulates of the theory of employment, namely, that the wage rate is equal to the marginal product of labor.

"In emphasising our point of departure from the classical system, we must not overlook an important point of agreement. For we shall maintain the first postulate as heretofore, subject only to the same qualifications as in classical theory; and we must pause, for a moment, to consider what this involves.

It means that with a given organization, equipment and technique, real wage and the volume of output (and hence of employment) are uniquely correlated, so that, in general, an increase in employment can only occur to the accompaniment of a decline in the rate of real wages. Thus I am not disputing this vital fact which the classical economists have (rightly) asserted as indefeasible. (...) Thus if employment increases, then, in the short period, the reward per unit of labour in terms of wage goods must, in general, decline and profits increase. This is simply the observe of the familiar proposition that industry is normally working subject to decreasing returns in the short period during which equipment etc. is assumed to be constant; so that the marginal product in the wage-good industries (which governs real wage) necessarily diminishes as employment is increased. So long, indeed, as this proposition holds, *any* means of increasing employment must lead at the same time to a diminution of the marginal product and hence of the rate of wages measured in terms of this product." (Keynes, 1967, p. 17.)

Thus it appears that Keynes did in fact have in mind a price equilibrium situation when he discussed the wage employment relation, and Patinkin

(1965) could write that "the involuntary unemployment of the *General Theory* need *not* have its origin in wage rigidities. Indeed, in this respect, we are more Keynesians than Keynes" (p. 340).

III. Inventories

If the product of the firm is storeable, the analysis in the preceding section is not entirely satisfactory, at least not in the quantity equilibrium case. Although the absence of demand will prevent the firm from selling the desired volume at the given market price, it does not prevent the firm from producing for stock. Moreover, if the firm has accumulated inventories earlier, it can satisfy demand either from stock or from output. In these cases, the value of the marginal product is not determined by the state of effective demand.

In the following discussion, the employment decision will be considered from the inventory management point of view.

Inventory management decisions are of necessity intertemporal and thus the profit maximization principle is not a sufficient criterion as such, since the firm has to compare profits in different periods. A natural extension of the profit maximization principle is the maximization of present value, i.e. the sum of the discounted profits of the firm. The discount factor R^{-1} is assumed to be a given constant, less than one but greater than zero; it is governed by the market rate of interest, $r = R - 1$.

Decisions are assumed to be made at one point in time, and both the expectations and the equipment (including inventories) of the firm are taken as predetermined variables in the analysis.

It is assumed that if the firm has an inventory S in the beginning of the decision period (prior to any transaction), then the inventory in the beginning of the next period is $S_{+1} = S + f(L) - Y$; in other words, the product is assumed to be perfectly storeable. In the literature on inventory management, the level of inventory holdings is sometimes allowed to be negative, which can be regarded as capturing the effect of unfilled orders. In this paper the firm is assumed to lose orders which it cannot satisfy, and the lowest value of S is taken to be zero: $S \geqslant 0$.

The present value of the firm in the beginning of the *next* period depends, *inter alia*, on S_{+1} and on the firm's future employment policy. The maximum of this present value, achieved by employing the best policy from the next period and onwards, is denoted by $V_{+1}(S_{+1})$. The function $V_{+1}(\cdot)$, which for each value of S_{+1} indicates the present value obtainable, is assumed to be given in this section. Moreover, it is assumed that this function has continuous derivatives

$$V'_{+1}(\cdot) > 0 \quad \text{and} \quad V''_{+1}(\cdot) < 0$$

for positive values of the argument.

When the firm employs L units of labor in the first period and from then on implements the best employment policy, its present value at the beginning of the decision period is

$$Y - wL + R^{-1}V_{+1}(S + f(L) - Y).$$

The first period profit is $Y - wL$ and the discounted value of future profits $R^{-1}V_{+1}(S_{+1})$. We assume that there are no costs of carrying over inventory from one period to the next, and as $S_{+1} = S + f(L) - Y$, the formula follows.

Optimum L is again denoted by L^*, and, correspondingly $S^*_{+1} = S + f(L^*) - Y$. Whenever S^*_{+1} and L^* are (strictly) positive, they satisfy the marginal optimality condition

$$w = R^{-1}V'_{+1}(S^*_{+1})f'(L^*). \tag{3}$$

The optimum decision is to equate the marginal cost of production $w/f'(L)$ with the marginal value of the product $R^{-1}V'_{+1}(S_{+1})$. This is subject to the qualification that S_{+1} cannot be reduced below zero. In the boundary case $S^*_{+1} = 0$ it is required that

$$Y = f(L^*) + S \quad \text{and} \quad w \geqslant R^{-1}V'_{+1}(0)f'(L^*).$$

Eq. (3) implicitly defines L^* as a function of S. Taking the derivatives with respect to S on both sides of (3) and cancelling out the term R^{-1}, we get

$$0 = V''_{+1}(S^*_{+1})(1 + df(L^*)/dS)f'(L^*) + V_{+1}(S^*_{+1})f''(L^*)dL^*/dS.$$

The last equation implies

$$-1 < \frac{df(L^*)}{dS} < 0. \tag{4}$$

A *ceteris paribus* increase in inventories reduces output but not by the entire amount of the increase in stocks, presupposing that S is positive since, otherwise, no reduction is possible.

Let $V(S)$ be the highest present value the firm can achieve when it initially has an inventory S. We have

$$V(S) = \max_{L} [Y - wL + R^{-1}V_{+1}(S_{+1})]$$
$$= Y - wL^* + R^{-1}V_{+1}(S^*_{+1}).$$

When $S^*_{+1} > 0$, the derivative of the present value with respect to S can be worked out as follows:

$$V'(S) = \frac{\partial[Y - wL^* + R^{-1}V_{+1}(S + f(L^*) - Y)]}{\partial S} + \frac{\partial[\qquad]}{\partial L^*}\frac{dL^*}{dS} = \frac{\partial[\qquad]}{\partial S}$$

(by the optimality condition)

$$= R^{-1}V'_{+1}(S^*_{+1});$$

the discounted marginal value of the (optimum) inventory tomorrow is equal to the marginal value of inventory today:

$$V'(S) = R^{-1}V'_{+1}(S^*_{+1}). \tag{5}$$

Substituting $V'(S)$ for $R^{-1}V'_{+1}(S^*_{+1})$ in the optimality condition (3) above, gives

$$w = V'(S)f'(L^*). \tag{6}$$

The wage rate is equal to the marginal physical product of labor multiplied by the marginal value (or shadow price) of the product. It would seem that when the inventory holding occurs, $S^*_{+1} > 0$, there is no need to abandon the classical postulate that the wage is equal to the marginal product of labor. But this postulate has to be interpreted.

It is useful to recall that Keynes used the concept "classical" in a broad sense, and in it he included the concept "neoclassical". The core of the neoclassical theory shows that prices in equilibrium measure physical transformation opportunities available to the economy, or to turn it the other way around, that equilibrium prices are determined by the technology of producers and the preferences of households. The correct interpretation is no doubt eq. (1). However, there is no reason why the "marginal product of labor" could not be interpreted as a value concept, and in view of the fact that neither labor nor products of labor are measurable in common physical units of economic interest, this may even be a natural interpretation.

The value interpretation (6) of the postulate does not express the original neoclassical idea in a simplified form as (1) does. Instead, it is a much broader statement which allows for both the case where prices measure transformation opportunities and the opposite case. The classical postulate in value form, stripped of its neoclassical content, is generally valid whenever firms can purchase labor at a given wage rate. It does not follow, however, that it is an empty statement, for it implies that a reduction in the wage rate increases the demand for labor. In other words, an increase in employment can occur only if real wages fall—provided that everything else remains constant.

Only a change in w which leaves $V_{+1}(\cdot)$ unaffected will be considered.

The effect of a change in w on the present value of the firm (for a given value of S) can be calculated as

$$\frac{\partial V}{\partial w} = \frac{\partial[Y - wL^* + R^{-1}V_{+1}(S + f(L^*) - Y)]}{\partial w} + \frac{\partial[\quad\quad]}{\partial L^*} \cdot \frac{\partial L^*}{\partial w}$$

(the effect of a change in w on Y is excluded)

$$= \frac{\partial [\qquad\qquad]}{\partial w} \quad \text{(by the optimality condition)}$$

$$= -L^*.$$

The only effect of a change in the wage rate on the present value of the firm is the direct cost effect.

It is assumed that the derivatives $\partial^2 V/\partial S \partial w$ and $\partial^2 V/\partial w \partial S$ are continuous and thus identical; then

$$\frac{\partial^2 V}{\partial w \partial S} = \frac{\partial^2 V}{\partial S \partial w} = -\frac{\partial L^*}{\partial S}$$

which is, in accordance with the earlier notation, $-dL^*/dS$.

It is now easy to set forth the inverse relation between employment offered and the wage rate.

Returning to eq. (6) and taking the derivative with respect to w on both sides, gives

$$1 = \frac{\partial V'(S)}{\partial w} f'(L^*) + V'(S) f''(L^*) \frac{\partial L^*}{\partial w}$$

$$= -\frac{\partial L^*}{\partial S} f'(L^*) + V'(S) f''(L^*) \frac{\partial L^*}{\partial w}$$

$$= -\frac{\partial f(L^*)}{\partial S} + V'(S) f''(L^*) \frac{\partial L^*}{\partial w}$$

or

$$\frac{\partial L^*}{\partial w} = \frac{1 + \partial f(L^*)/\partial S}{V'(S) f''(L^*)}.$$

As the numerator is positive, through (4), and the denominator negative, $\partial L^*/\partial w$ is negative.

It is not difficult to see that an increase in effective demand Y (in such a way that $V_{+1}(\cdot)$ is left unchanged) increases the demand for labor as much as a reduction of equal size in S or

$$\frac{\partial L^*}{\partial Y} = -\frac{\partial L^*}{\partial S},$$

provided that $S > 0$.

Inequalities (4) say that a change in effective demand is only partly reflected by a change in output, as part of it is absorbed in the building up or depletion of inventories. It is only in the limiting case $\partial f(L^*)/\partial Y = 1$ that effective demand is fully reflected in output.

The same limiting case is also the only exception to the general dependence of the demand for labor on the wage rate. It can be concluded that the quantity equilibrium analysis in Section II is only applicable as such in the case where $\partial f(L^*)/\partial Y = 1$. When inventory holding serves as an alternative outlet for output, or for the intermediate values of $\partial f(L^*)/\partial Y$, it appears that the crucial feature of quantity equilibrium situations need not be the price insensitivity of employment decisions (although the elasticities are not the same as in price equilibrium analysis). Although the sales constraint prevents the firm from adjusting its position on the market, inventory holding offers the firm a new perspective so that room for choice remains.[1]

To round out this picture of quantity equilibrium, buttressed by inventory holdings, it can be noted that *from an economic point of view* the firm regards output sold and output stored as different goods, although they share the same physical properties. However, they are substitutes; and their substitutability is indicated by the difference between the market price 1 and the imputed price $V'(S)$. The nature of this substitutability is explored in more detail in the next section. It is not possible to derive $V'(S)$ by restricting attention to the decision period; the value of an inventory is determined by the events the firm expects to occur and by the decisions it will make (or expects itself to make) in the future. Thus the analysis is extended as far into the future as is required to determine the first period marginal value of the output.

IV. The Value of Output

It is necessary to present our assumptions about the firm's expectations in more detail. The variables are dated so that the subscript 0 refers to the (first) decision period and the subscript t to the tth period after that. Wage and sales expectations can then be represented as a sequence of variables w_t and Y_t, respectively.

It is still assumed that the firm experiences no uncertainty about its expectations. For simplicity, it is assumed in this section that the state of demand is expected to remain at Y until period $T-1$, after which the sales constraint is (at least temporarily) lifted, and that the expected wage rate settles down to a permanent level, w^*, before period T. At wage w^*, the sales constraint Y is assumed to be binding.

With subscripts added, eqs. (6) and (5) in the preceding section can be written $w_0 = V'(S_0)f'(L_0^*)$ and $V_0'(S_0) = R^{-1}V_1'(S_1^*)$. If the firm expects itself to make optimal employment decisions in the future, these relations generalize readily to[2]

$$w_t = V_t'(S_t^*)f'(L_t^*) \tag{6'}$$

---

[1] As noted by Barro & Grossman in their recent book (1976, p. 92, footnote 41); however, the authors do not carry their analysis beyond this footnote.

[2] A continuous time treatment would have yielded the transversality condition below in a slightly more elegant form, but on the other hand, it is easier to make allowances for uncertainty in discrete time. See for example the articles by Karlin in Arrow et al. (1958).

and

$$V_t'(S_t^*) = R^{-1}V_{t+1}'(S_{t+1}^*).$$ (5')

It follows that

$$\frac{w_t}{f'(L_t^*)} = R^{-1}\frac{w_{t+1}}{f'(L_{t+1}^*)}.$$ (7)

In the optimum plan the planned marginal cost of production increases geometrically in the same way as R^t. This holds true as long as S_{t+1}^* is positive.

The first period value of output is not known in advance, and has to be determined somehow. Whenever the next period marginal value is known, this can be done with the help of eq. (5). The causation then runs in reverse order, from the future to the present. The recursive equation in (5') defers the "final" determination of the marginal value of output; it follows from it that

$$V_0'(S_0) = R^{-t}V_t'(S_t^*).$$

What is needed is a base point, a date in the future which can be used to determine the marginal value independently. As the recursive relations remain valid as long as the firm holds some inventories, there is no hope of finding the base point before the stocks are exhausted.

After period $T-1$, the firm does not hold inventories, and in the optimum plan we have

$$S_T^* = 0.$$

It is conceivable that inventories are depleted even before T, but this possibility is not considered here; T is the first period for which $S_T^* = 0$.

The optimum plan consists of two phases. During the first phase (the adjustment) the firm holds positive inventories, which on the average are being depleted; the demand for labor is governed by the recursive relations. During the second phase the inventory is exhausted and the optimum decision is to equate sales with output so that the market value of the marginal product of labor is equal to the wage rate w^*.

All that remains is to piece the two phases together. This can be done in the usual manner, by requiring that the present value be maximized with respect to L_{T-1}.

L_{T-1}^* cannot be larger than L_T^*, for otherwise

$$S_T^* = S_{T-1}^* + f(L_{T-1}^*) - Y > S_{T-1}^* + f(L_{T-1}^*) - f(L_T^*)$$

(the constraint Y is binding at wage $w^* = f'(L_T^*)$)

$$> 0 \quad \text{if } L_{T-1}^* > L_T^*$$

which contradicts $S_T^* = 0$. Thus

$$f'(L_T^*) \leqslant f'(L_{T-1}^*).$$

If, on the other hand, $w_{T-1}/f'(L_{T-1})$ is smaller than $R^{-1}w_T/f'(L_T)$, the firm can increase its present value by planning to produce an extra unit of output in period $T-1$ and reducing production in period T, that is to say, by accumulating a slight inventory for period T. Again this implies that S_T is positive, and thus

$$\frac{w_{T-1}}{f'(L_{T-1}^*)} \geqslant R^{-1}\frac{w_T}{f'(L_T^*)}.$$

As w_{T-1} and w_T are both equal to w^*, it follows that

$$f'(L_{T-1}^*) \leqslant Rf'(L_T^*).$$

The two inequalities together can be written as the transversality condition

$$f'(L_T^*) \leqslant f'(L_{T-1}^*) \leqslant Rf'(L_T^*).$$

When the unit period is short, R is approximately equal to one and the inequalities reduce, in essence, to the requirement that the marginal cost of production should not jump at the end of adjustment.

This continuity requirement can be written

$$f'(L_{T-1}^*) = Rf'(L_T^*). \tag{8}$$

Eq. (8) provides the required base point, and it follows that

$$V_0'(S_0) = R^{-T}\frac{w_T}{f'(L_T^*)}.$$

Since the marginal cost of production is equal to the market price of the product in the long run, we have $V_0'(S_0) = R^{-T}$, or to return to the notation in the preceding section:

$$V'(S) = R^{-T}.$$

T is the time needed to deplete the initial inventory S entirely. It cannot be negative, and for a positive rate of interest, the shadow price of the output never exceeds the market price. The longer the time needed for adjustment, the lower the shadow price.

Two valid explanations for a difference between 1 and R^{-T} are excluded from the analysis by assumption, namely expected changes in market prices and storage costs (including all changes in the quality of the product resulting from storing); so a third one is required.

No generality is lost if it is assumed that in every period the last unit of output goes into stock and is not sold until the last period of adjustment $T-1$.

The product of the last worker employed in the decision period has to remain in stock for T periods before it is sold, although it still has to bring the firm the positive rate of return obtainable in the capital market. Through a sufficient decrease in the amount of labor employed, the firm can reduce the marginal cost of production; when the amount of employment offered is low enough, labor (as embodied in stored output) becomes attractive as an asset.

It follows that any amount of labor can be employed if the wage rate is low enough, but the argument requires that the marginal cost of production respond to changes in the rate of employment. When input–output coefficients are fixed and labor is the only factor which limits production, the marginal cost of production is constant and nothing is gained by producing for stock. The firm will not build up inventories during periods of slack demand and deplete them when demand is brisk; instead, output will move *pari passu* with sales, independently of wages, wage expectations, sales expectations, discount rates, etc. If for some unexplained reason the firm happens to have a positive amount of output in stock, inventory will be depleted before any new production takes place and the demand for labor will be zero during the inventory adjustment process, for all positive wage rates.[1]

V. Conclusion

The introduction of inventories into the basic Barro–Grossman model opens a number of interesting avenues, some of which have been explored above. It appears that a sharp distinction between price and quantity equilibrium is not justified if the inventory holding motive is operative. The wage rate, the rate of interest and the state of effective demand are all determinants of the demand for labor and consequently, even under Keynesian conditions, unemployment can be influenced through any of these three channels. This is in part illustrated by conclusions (i) and (ii) in the Introduction. However, it should be stressed that the assumed independence of sales and wage expectations from changes in current wages and in current demand more or less limits the field of macro-economic applications for these specific conclusions.

A reduction in wages results in increased unemployment if it leads to a decrease in sales or to expectations of further reductions in wages on such a scale that the imputed value of current output declines more than in proportion to the decrease in wages. It does not follow from conclusion (i) that unemployment is best prevented by making (real) wages sufficiently flexible.[2]

---

[1] Grandmont & Laroque (1975) treated the issue of the positivity of wages in Keynesian equilibrium. They concluded that a zero wage level may be required for the equilibrium—even if the (physical) marginal product of labor is positive—when sales expectations are pessimistic. In view of the present analysis, these cases require either that prospects are very poor (roughly, the special case $Y = 0$, $T = \infty$ which has been bypassed above) or that the law of diminishing returns does not apply with respect to labor.

[2] Keynes, of course, placed considerable emphasis on the negative repercussions of wage reductions on the demand for labor in Chapter 19 of the *General Theory*, entitled, somewhat misleadingly "Changes in Money Wages".

References

Arrow, K. J., Karlin, S. & Scarf, H.: *Studies in the mathematical theory of inventory and production.* Stanford, California, 1958.

Barro, R. J. & Grossman, H.: A general disequilibrium model of income and employment. *American Economic Review*, March 1971.

Barro, R. J. & Grossman, H.: *Money, employment and inflation.* USA, 1976.

Grandmont, J. M. & Laroque, G.: On temporary Keynesian equilibria. *Review of Economic Studies*, October 1975.

Keynes, J. M.: *The general theory of employment, interest and money.* Great Britain, 1967.

Leijonhufvud, A.: Effective demand failures. *The Swedish Journal of Economics*, March 1973.

Patinkin, D.: *Money, interest and prices.* USA, 1965.

THE INTERACTION BETWEEN MULTIPLIER AND INFLATION PROCESSES[1]

Claes-Henric Siven

University of Stockholm, Stockholm, Sweden

Abstract

The Barro–Grossman theory of the demand and the supply multiplier is generalized in the following ways: Household behavior under disequilibrium is derived from the knowledge of the behavior under equilibrium using the Tobin–Houthakker theory of rationing. The setting of prices and wages under equilibrium and disequilibrium conditions is analyzed. It is shown that the value of the demand multiplier depends on whether employment is instantaneously adjusted during a depression. The results of the microeconomic analysis are used for constructing a macroeconomic model where the interactions between inflation and quantitative adjustments are studied.

I. Introduction

Patinkin's analysis of involuntary unemployment (Patinkin, 1965) and Clower's analysis of the consumption function (Clower, 1965) implied that the fundamental macroeconomic behavior equations were derived from preference theory, even though assumptions different from the neo-classical ones were made concerning the transaction possibilities of individual firms and households. Barro Grossman brought together the results of Patinkin and Clower in a general disequilibrium theory (Barro & Grossman, 1971).

The analysis of Barro and Grossman is limited however by the assumption that the price system is fixed. Not only does this imply that the Barro–Grossman modernization of multiplier theory does not permit the analysis of the relationship between inflation and unemployment, it also means that preference theory stops short of price-setting and wage-setting decisions.[2] The

---

unexpected high rate of wage inflation with getting comparative good wage offers and
[1] I am grateful to Karl-Gustaf Löfgren for comments on an earlier version of this paper. An extended version of the paper was presented at the European Meeting of the Econometric Society in Helsinki in 1976. The report is financed by the Bank of Sweden Tercentenary Foundation.
[2] This is in contrast to the theory of the Phillips curve where the pricing and wage setting processes are explicitly analysed and where the interaction between inflation and unemployment stands in the center of the interest. A difficulty with this analysis is, however, that unemployment in a certain sense is voluntary, resulting from the fact that the unemployed have certain minimum requirements for the jobs they will accept. Variations in the rate of unemployment are caused by the job seekers misinterpreting an unexpectedly high rate of wage inflation as comparatively good wage offers and

purpose of the present paper is to take the natural step of integrating the analysis of household behavior under general excess supply and general excess demand with the setting of prices and wages by firms. These decisions are analyzed in a dynamic context where all prices and wages are expected to rise by the expected rate of inflation; the actual rate of inflation will fluctuate during different phases of the business cycle around this expected rate, which is backed up by monetary expansion.

The assumptions of the present analysis are basically the same as those of Barro & Grossman. Two important changes should be noted, however. The first is that both households and firms expect prices and wage rates to change over time. The second concerns the manner in which prices and wages are determined. Firms are no longer price takers, but have some monopoly power in the goods market and some monopsony power in the labor market. Prices and wage rates are imperfectly flexible (but *not* inflexible) due to the fact that the firms' expectations concerning the level of demand for goods and labor supply lag behind the actual development.

II. Household Planning in Equilibrium, under Keynesian Underemployment and under General Excess Demand

The following analysis will by and large start from the same premises as those of Barro & Grossman. An important new aspect, however, is that endogenously explained inflation may exist and that households expect rising price and wage levels. Hence the planning problem of the household is to determine the value of its suply of labor, x^S, its consumption, y^D, and its real balances at the end of the planning period, $(M/P + m^D) R$,[1] so as to maximize the utility function $U(x^S, y^D, (M/P + m^D) R)$ subject to the budget equation, $\pi + wx^S + m^S - y^D - m^D = 0$, and possibly to some additonal restriction; π denotes total real profits (assumed to be distributed to the households), $w = W/P$ is the real wage rate, and m^S is an exogenously given increase of the real supply of money that may be thought of as the net of lump sum transfers to the household and its lump sum tax payments. The utility function is assumed to possess the usual concavity properties. The only way in which the household takes the future beyond the planning period into condsideration is by attaching utility to the real value of initial balances in the subsequent period. The household may save by increasing its real balances. If the price level is expected to increase by ΔP^e, the household receives a negative interest rate on cash balances, the factor of discount being $1 : (1 + \Delta P^e/P)$.

---

thus accepting employment offers which they would not normally consider. In the same way an unexpected wage deflation leads to fewer acceptances of wage offers and thus to increasing unemployment. Cf. Phelps (1970), especially the articles by Holt, Phelps, Phelps–Winter, and Mortensen. Cf. also Siven (1975).

[1] Here M/P denotes initial real balances, m^D increases of real balances during the period, and R is a measure of the *expected* increase of the price level, $R = 1 : (1 + \Delta P^e/P)$.

II.1. *Household Planning in Equilibrium*

In equilibrium, the household plans as to maximize the Lagrange expression

$$L = U(x^S, y^D, (M/P + m^D) R) + \lambda_1(\pi + wx^S + m^S - y^D - m^D) \tag{1}$$

By differentiating (1) with respect to the control variables the first order conditions for an inner maximum are obtained. Total differentiation of the first order conditions will then give the control variables as functions of the exogenous variables. It is easy to show that the effects of the exogenous variables may be split up into substitution, income, and real balance effects. If leisure, goods and increases of real balances are all substitutes and superior goods, the behavioral equations and the signs of the partial derivatives are as follows:[1]

$$x^S = x^S\left(w, 1, R, \pi + x_0^S w + m^S, \left(\frac{M}{P} + m_0^D\right) R\right), \quad x_5^S = x_4^S$$
$$ + \; - \; + - -$$

$$y^D = y^D\left(w, 1, R, \pi + x_0^S w + m^S, \left(\frac{M}{P} + m_0^D\right) R\right), \quad y_5^D = y_4^D$$
$$ + \; - \; - + +$$

$$m^D = m^D\left(w, 1, R, \pi + x_0^S w + m^S, \left(\frac{M}{P} + m_0^D\right) R\right), \quad m_5^D = m_4^D - 1 \tag{2}$$
$$ + \; + \; + + -$$

Here x_0^S denotes the supply of labor before a disturbance and m_0^D denotes the flow demand for real balances before a disturbance. The second argument of each equation is unity since the budget equation has been expressed in real terms. Variations in P are thus not separately noted but contained in variations in the real wage rate, w. x_5^S denotes the derivative with respect to the fifth argument and x_4^S with respect to the fourth argument of the first equation.

An increase of real balances, M/P, will be used partly for consumption (cf. the second equation), partly to increase final real balances. But at the same time, this will imply a decreased flow demand for real balances.

An increased real wage rate will affect household behavior via a substitution effect (the first argument of each equation) and an income effect (the fourth argument). For labor supply these effects work in different directions. Following Barro & Grossman, it is assumed that the substitution effect dominates so that the supply of labor curve will have a positive slope with respect to the real wage rate.

It should be noted that the behavior equations (2) are homogeneous of degree zero in the absolute price level, the absolute wage level, and initial nominal monetary balances. This is not the case with respect to an increased

---

[1] Note that x_0^S and m_0^D should not be interpreted as arguments; i.e. the system (1) should not be regarded as behavior equations in the usual sense, but as equations describing the effects on the endogenous variables of changes in the exogenous variables w, R, π, m^S and M/P. The same applies, *mutatis mutandis*, to the interpretation of equations (4) and (6).

expected rate of wage and price inflation. An increased rate of expected inflation coupled to an equiproportional increase of the flow supply of nominal balances will, via the substitution effect, increase the demand for goods and decrease the flow demand for real balances.

II.2. *Household Planning under Keynesian Underemployment*

Now assume that there is no longer equilibrium in all markets, or more specifically, that there is excess supply in the labor market. At the given real wage rate the household is no longer in a position to sell the desired number of hours of labor. An extra restriction puts an upper limit on the possible number of labor hours per period. It is this upper limit which may lead to involuntary underemployment.

The planning problem of the household which is underemployed can be formulated as follows. The values of the control variables (supply of labor hours, consumption demand, and flow demand for real balances) should be chosen so as to maximize the utility function subject to the budget equation and to the additional (rationing) constraint requiring the supply of labor to equal demand. Hence the function to be maximized is the Lagrangean:

$$L' = U(x^{S'}, y^{D'}, (M/P + m^{D'}) R) + \lambda_1'(\pi + wx^{S'} + m^S - y^{D'} - m^{D'}) + \lambda_2'(x^D - x^{S'}) \, (1)$$

$$(3)$$

where the control variables and the Lagrange multipliers are denoted by a prime to show that their values are now chosen subject to an additional restraint.

The first order conditions for an (interior) maximum may now be obtained. It should be pointed out that the Lagrange multiplier for the rationing restriction may be given an interesting economic interpretation since λ_2'/λ_1' shows how much the real wage rate would have to be decreased in order to induce the household freely to supply the amount of labor which the rationing restriction now forces it to choose. It is in that case assumed that the income effect of the decreased real wage rate is compensated for.

Total differentiation of the maximum conditions gives the following behavior equations for the underemployed household:

$$x^{S'} = x^{S'}\left(w, 1, R, \pi + x_0^{S'} w + m^S, \left(\frac{M}{P} + m_0^{D'}\right) R, x^D\right)$$
$$\quad\;\; 0 \;\; 0 \;\; 0 \qquad 0 \qquad\qquad\quad 0 \qquad\quad +$$

$$y^{D'} = y^{D'}\left(w, 1, R, \pi + x_0^{S'} w + m^S, \left(\frac{M}{P} + m_0^{D'}\right) R, x^D\right)$$
$$\quad\;\; 0 \;\; - \;\; - \qquad + \qquad\qquad\quad + \qquad\quad +$$

$$m^{D'} = m^{D'}\left(w, 1, R, \pi + x_0^{S'} w + m^S, \left(\frac{M}{P} + m_0^{D'}\right) R, x^D\right) \qquad (4)$$
$$\quad\;\;\; 0 \;\; + \;\; + \qquad + \qquad\qquad\quad - \qquad\quad +$$

---

[1] Note that the unchanged form of the utility function (with respect to $(M/P + m^{D'}) R$) implies that the household expects that there will be equilibrium in the next period.

where $y_5^{D'} = y_4^{D'}$ and $m_5^{D'} = m_4^{D'} - 1$. As long as the rationing restriction is binding, $x_6^{S'} = 1$.

In ascertaining the signs of the partial derivatives of the behavior equations use has been made of the theory of rationing.[1] The effect on the demand for goods of an increased demand for labor hours (the spill-over effect) is equal to the ratio between the substitution effect on the demand for goods and the substitution effect on the supply of labor of an increased wage level. An analogous expression holds for the effect on the flow demand for real cash balances:

$$\frac{\partial y^{D'}}{\partial x^D} = \frac{y_1^D}{x_1^S} > 0, \quad \frac{\partial m^{D'}}{\partial x^D} = \frac{m_1^D}{x_1^S} > 0 \ (2) \tag{4a}$$

The denominator, x_1^S, is always negative. The sign of the spill-over effect then depends on whether goods and leisure are substitutes (positive effect) or complements (negative effect). The intuitive interpretation of this is the following. If two goods are substitutes, a decrease of the first good, leisure, means that the demand for the second good will increase; note that the decrease of leisure implies that the number of labor hours increases. The same reasoning applies to the flow demand for real balances.

The theory of rationing also implies the following equations which compare the effects in equilibrium with the effects when there is involuntary underemployment:

$$y_i^{D'} = y_i^D - \frac{\partial y^{D'}}{\partial x^D} x_i^S, \ m_i^{D'} = m_i^D - \frac{\partial m^{D'}}{\partial x^D} x_i^S \ (3) \quad i = 1, \dots, 6 \tag{4b}$$

For $i = 4$ the interpretation of 4b is that the effect of an increased income on the demand for goods at underemployment (= the marginal propensity to consume) is equal to the income effect in eqilibrium minus the effect of an increased demand for labor hours on the demand for goods (= the spill-over effect), times the effect on the supply of labor of an increased income in equilibrium. The economic significance of this is that the income effect on the demand for goods where there is underemployment partly depends on the equilibrium income effect, partly on an indirect effect working in the following way. An increased income would, in equilibrium, imply a decreased supply of labor. Since the supply of labor is now fixed at the level determined by the rationing constraint (= the insufficient demand for labor), the increased income will instead imply that the rationing constraint is not as severe as before. This has the same effect on the demand for goods as an increased

---

[1] Cf. Tobin–Houthakker (1950–51).
[2] It should be noted that these connections are of a local nature. It will be assumed, however, that they approximately hold for interlocal comparisons.
[3] It should be noted that these relationships are of a local nature. It will be assumed, however, that they hold approximately for comparisons in the large.

demand for labor, and thus works via the spill-over effect. Analogous reasoning applies to the effect on the flow demand for real balances in underemployment (= the marginal propensity to save).

True, the effects on consumption and saving of an increased income (e.g. increase of π) have the same sign as an increased employment. However, the magnitudes are generally different: $Y_4^{D'} \neq wy_6^{D'}$ and $m_4^{D'} \neq wm_6^{D'}$. This is to say that the effects of increased household incomes will differ according as they are generated by increased distributed profits or increased transfers on the one hand or by an increased employment on the other hand. In the latter case the increased income will be coupled to decreased leisure, and that will generally affect the choice, in a way that depends upon whether leisure and other goods are substitutes or complements.

By using (2) and (4 b) it is possible to show that the marginal propensity to consume, $y_4^{D'}$, is positive and greater than the income effect in equilibrium, y_4^{D}. In the same way one can show that the marginal propensity to save, $m_4^{D'}$, is greater than the equilibrium income effect on the flow demand for cash balances, m_4^{D}. This is because of that the supply of labor will decrease if the income increases in equilibrium, but not when there is underemployment. Consequently, more room is left for increases in consumption and saving when there is underemployment.

II.3. *Household Planning under General Excess Demand*

The household is now free to vary its supply of labor. However there is excess demand in the goods market. This means that there is an upper limit to the quantity of goods which the household may buy during the period. Accordingly we assume that the household behaves as if it maximized utility subject to budget constraint as well as to an additional constraint:

$$L'' = U(x^{S''}, y^{D''}, (M/P + m^{D''}) R) + \lambda_1''(\pi + wx^{S''} + m^S - y^{D''} - m^{D''}) + \lambda_2''(y^S - y^{D''})\,^1$$

(5)

where a double prime sign is affixed to the control variables and Lagrange multipliers to indicate that the optimization is done under conditions such that the household at given prices wants to buy more goods than it is able to do.

From the first order maximum conditions one may note the following interpretation of λ_2''/λ_1'': if the present goods price is increased by that amount, the household would wish to buy the amount of goods which the rationing constraint now forces it to buy. The income effect of the price increase is in that case assumed to be compensated for.

---

[1] The fact that the form of the utility function is unchanged relative to the case of equilibrium planning implies that the household expects that there will be equilibrium in the next period.

Total differentiation of the first order maximum conditions gives the following behavior equations:

$$x^{S''} = x^{S''}\left(w, 1, R, \pi + x_0^{S''}w + m^S, \left(\frac{M}{P} + m_0^{D''}\right)R, y^S\right)$$
$$+\ 0\ +\qquad\qquad -\qquad\quad -\qquad +$$

$$y^{D''} = y^{D''}\left(w, 1, R, \pi + x_0^{S''}w + m^S, \left(\frac{M}{P} + m_0^{D''}\right)R, y^S\right)$$
$$0\ 0\ 0\qquad\qquad 0\qquad\qquad 0\qquad +$$

$$m^{D''} = m^{D''}\left(w, 1, R, \pi + x_0^{S''}w + m^S, \left(\frac{M}{P} + m_0^{D''}\right)R, y^S\right) \tag{6}$$
$$+\ 0\ +\qquad\qquad +\qquad\qquad -\qquad -$$

where $x_5^{S''} = x_4^{S''}$ and $m_5^{D''} = m_4^{D''} - 1$. As long as the rationing restriction is binding, $y_6^{D''} = 1$.

As for the case of household planning under Keynesian underemployment, rationing theory may be used to derive the signs of the partial derivatives of the behavior equations. The effect on the supply of labor of an increased supply of goods (the spill-over effect $x_6^{S''}$) is found to be equal to the ratio between the equilibrium substitution effects on the supply of labor and the demand for goods of a price increase. The economic interpretation is that if leisure and consumption are substitutes, a less severe rationing constraint on consumption will increase consumption and, consequently, decrease leisure. This means that the supply of labor increases if, at the given price system, the supply of goods is increased. There is an analogous expression and economic interpretation for the flow demnd for real balances:

$$\frac{\partial x^{S''}}{\partial y^S} = \frac{x_2^S}{y_2^D} > 0, \quad \frac{\partial m^{D''}}{\partial y^S} = \frac{m_2^D}{y_2^D} < 0 \tag{6a}$$

Furthermore, each of the partial derivatives of the household behavior equations under general excess demand may be expressed in terms of the partial derivatives of the behavior equations in equilibrium:

$$x_i^{S''} = x_i^S - \frac{\partial x^{S''}}{\partial y^S} y_i^D, \quad m_i^{D''} = m_i^D - \frac{\partial m^{D''}}{\partial y^S} y_i^D; \quad i = 1, \ldots, 6 \tag{6b}$$

The economic interpretation of this expression is analogous to that of (4b). As for the case of Keynesian underemployment, (6a) and (6b) are local conditions, holding exactly if the rationing restriction is on the verge of being binding. Also in the present case we assume that (6a) and (6b) approximately hold for comparisons in the large.

III. The Behavior of the Firm

In the Barro–Grossman model the price system is exogenously given. Firms are quantity adjusters and the price system is determined "by the market". There are three disadvantages to this assumption: it is not very realistic; it makes it impossible to explain endogenously the inflation process as a result of the interaction of the setting of prices and wages by rational individual agents; and it is inconsistent with the fact that perfect competition can only exist in equilibrium.[1]

It is assumed that only firms determine prices and wage rates. Labor unions are abstracted from. To simplify, it is assumed that the firms need not take the possibility of a changing number of customers or employees into consideration when determining their prices and wage rates.[2] The slope of the demand curve for the firm's product (which, for analytical convenience, is assumed not to be storable) then only represents the fact that the quantity each customer demands will change when the price changes. The same reasoning applies to wage changes. Even if the price and wage setting of a firm is not affected by the prices and wages of the other firms via the competitive process, there is still an influence since the customers of one firm are employees of other firms. The demand for a given firm's product is thus affected by the wage setting of the other firms. In the same way, the employees of that firm are customers of other firms. If the other firms change their prices, the supply of labor, which the firm is confronted by, will change.

The number of households is assumed to be considerably greater than the number of firms, which is assumed to be "very large". All households and all firms are identical. This means that the aggregates may be represented by a representative household and a representative firm, respectively. To keep down the number of notations, no notational distinction will be made between e.g. the demand curve of an individual household, the sum of the demand curves of the customers of a certain firm, or the agregate demand curve for goods of the economy.

In the beginning of each period the firm sets the price and the wage rate which it expects will maximize profits.

Profits are maximized subject to the production function $y^{Se} = F(x^{De})$,

---

[1] Cf. Arrow (1959).

[2] This is in contrast to the theory of the Phillips curve derived by Holt, Phelps and Mortensen (cf. Phelps, 1970 and Siven, 1975) where friction in the goods and labor markets together with the competitive process where firms try to attract customers and employees from each other stand in the center of the analysis. The imperfect overview of the market and the search processes resulting from this imperfect knowledge are not only of fundamental importance for this type of construction of macromodels describing the interaction between inflation and unemployment, they also mark one of the more important hypothesis of Arrow's pathbreaking paper on price adjustment (Arrow (1959). This hypothesis as yet remains unexplored. It may form one building block in the future work on integrating the Barro–Grossman theory of multiplier processes and the theory of the Phillips curve.

where index e denotes expected quantities; cf. below. The production function is assumed to have a positive first derivative and a negative second derivative. From the Lagrangean

$$L = Py^{De} - Wx^{Se} + \lambda(F(x^{Se}) - y^{De})$$ (7)

we derive the first order conditions for a maximum and the following behavior equations:[1]

$$P = P(y^{De}, x^{Se})$$
$$\quad + \ -$$

$$W = W(y^{De}, x^{Se})$$
$$\quad + \ -$$

$$\lambda = \lambda(y^{De}, x^{Se})$$ (8)
$$\quad + \ -$$

It is easy to show that the optimization will imply monopolistic behavior on the goods market and monopsonistic behavior on the labor market. The shadow price λ may be interpreted as the marginal cost.

In contrast to the case of perfect competition, it has not been possible to determine the direction of the effect on the real wage rate of variations in the demand for goods or in the supply of labor without further assumptions. It is assumed that the real wage rate will approximately be unaffected by variations of y^{De} and x^{Se}.

Prices and wage rates are set in the beginning of each period and are constant during the period. When determining the profit-maximizing price and wage rate, the firm bases its decision on what it expects to be the demand for its good, y^{De}, and the supply of labor, x^{Se}, during the period. These expectations are assumed to be *subjectively* certain. Since the firm expects prices and wage rates of other firms and nominal monetary balances to rise by the expected rate of inflation, $g^e = \Delta P^e/P^e = \Delta W^e/W^e = \Delta M^e/M^e$, and since the profit function and the Lagrangean (7) are both homogeneous of the first degree in P, P^e, W, W^e and M^e, the firm will first increase its price and wage rate in proportion to the expected rate of inflation.

In addition it may revise its expectations of the initial values of the level of demand for its product and the level of supply of labor hours by its employees (and this revision may indirectly reflect changed values of the firm's expectations of the prices and wage rates of the other firms). The total change from one period to another of the price and the wage rate of a certain firm may thus be written as:

---

[1] It should be observed that changes of the shift parameters of the behavior equations will determine *relative* changes of the price and wage rate.

$$\frac{\Delta P}{P} = g^e + \frac{\partial P}{\partial y^{De}} dy^{De} + \frac{\partial P}{\partial x^{Se}} dx^{Se}$$

$$\frac{\Delta W}{W} = g^e + \frac{\partial W}{\partial y^{De}} dy^{De} + \frac{\partial W}{\partial x^{Sw}} dx^{Se} \tag{9}$$

Despite the fact that firms are assumed to be subjectively certain of the level of demand in the coming period, they may be in error. And errors in their turn may provide one possible explanation of why there are changes of y^{De} and x^{Se}. If deviations between actual and expected levels of demand for goods and supply of labor hours, respectively, are recorded, these deviations will trigger adjustments of the firm's expectations for the next period:

$$\Delta y^{De} = \alpha(y^D - y^{De}), \quad \alpha > 0$$

$$\Delta x^{se} = \beta(x^S - x^{Se}), \quad \beta > 0 \tag{10}$$

where the expectations adjustment mechanism (10) does not include changes due to the expected rate of inflation, which are separately recorded. The adjustment mechanism (10) is too well-known to comment upon. However, one may note that the possibility of errors of forecast and the absence of an instantaneous adjustment of expectations actually imply that the firm acts in a stochastic environment and is aware of that fact. The consequences of this will be looked into in another context.[1]

IV. Macroeconomic Analysis

IV.1. *General Equilibrium*

General equilibrium implies a price system such that in each period there is equality between supply and demand simultaneously on each firm's goods and labor markets. Since the firms try to maximize profits, and since the maximization implies equilibrium, a necessary condition for equilibrium is that the individual firm has correct expectations about the demand curve for its product and the supply curve for labor of its employees. This implicitly presupposes a correct estimation of the shift parameters of the demand function for goods and the supply function for labor, *inter alia* the wage rates of the other firms (since the customers of the firm generally are employees of other firms) and the prices of the other firms (since the employees of the firm generally are customers of other firms). Since all firms and all households respectively are assumed to be identical, correct expectations of other firms' prices can be reduced to saying that a firm should decide on the price it expects other firms to set. Analogous reasoning holds for wage rates. The following system of equations describes the general equilibrium solution:

---

[1] Cf. Siven (1976).

$$y^D = y^{De}$$

$$x^S = x^{Se}$$

$$W = W(y^{De}, x^{Se})$$

$$P = P(y^{De}, x^{Se})$$

$$F(x^S) = y^D$$

$$\pi = y^D - wx^S$$

$$wx^S + \pi + m^S - y^D - m^D = 0$$

$$y^D = y^D \left(w, 1, R, \pi + wx_0^S + m^S, \left(\frac{M}{P} + m_0^D \right) R \right)$$

$$x^S = x^S \left(w, 1, R, \pi + wx_0^S + m^S, \left(\frac{M}{P} + m_0^D \right) R \right)$$

$$m^D = m^D \left(w, 1, R, \pi + wx_0^S + m^S, \left(\frac{M}{P} + m_0^D \right) R \right) \tag{11}$$

The first two equations of (11) are equilibrium conditions. The next two are the behavior equations of the firms, describing their wage and price setting. The fifth equation, stating that production of goods as a function of the supply of labor should be equal to the demand for goods, is implicit in the first four equations. This depends on the fact that profit maximization is subject to the restraint that production should equal demand for goods (note that the wage and price equations describe firm behavior when planned profits are maximized) and that firm expectations about the level of demand for goods and supply of labor are correct. The sixth equation defines aggregate profits. In addition it states that in equilibrium the demand for goods should equal national income (=aggregate profits plus wages). The seventh equation is the aggregate budget equation of the households. It is implicit in the last three equations, the behavior equations of the households, since household behavior is derived from utility maximization, which is done subject to the budget constraint. Furthermore, the aggregate budget equation is defined for general equilibrium. This depends on the fact that the household control parameters included in the budget equation are defined for planning under equilibrium conditions.

If the definition for aggregate profits is substituted into the aggregate budget equation the result is obtained that equilibrium on the goods and the labor market implies monetary equilibrium, $m^S - m^D = 0$. Equality between the flow supply and the flow demand for real balances implies that the households exactly plan to add the flow supply of money to their real balances. Since the flow supply of money is assumed to add to monetary balances by the same percent as the expected rate of inflation, the equality between flow supply and flow demand for real balances implies that the households plan to increase their nominal balances by the amount which is necessary for exactly compensating the effect on real balances of the expected higher price level in the next period.

Starting from a general equilibrium situation, increased initial monetary balances implies a new equilibrium situation where the wage level and the price level increase by the same percentage as initial nominal balances, cf. (11). This presupposes however that the expectations of the firms are instantaneously adjusted to the new situation. It is not only required that the firms immediately get information about the implications for consumer demand and labor supply of the increased nominal balances. The firms must also expect all other firms to adjust their prices and wage rates so that the new general equilibrium situation is instantly reached. This has to do with the fact mentioned before that the customers of a certain firm generally are employees of other firms and *vice versa*. If the firms are imperfectly informed about the magnitude of the shift of the household behavior equations or of the price and wage planning of the other firms, no instant equilibrating change of the price system is to be expected. The adjustment process will then partly woik through quantity changes to be discussed in the next two subsections.

IV.2. *Keynesian Underemployment*

The fact that the firms are not perfectly informed about the values of the shift parameters of the supply functions of their employees and the demand functions of their customers implies that they may overestimate or underestimate the demand for their products or the supply of labor by their employees. Now assume that erroneous expectations have led to prices and wages giving a correct real wage rate but too high a level of prices and wages. Hence initial real balances are too low. At the full-employment level of national income, the households therefore plan to increase their real balances by more than the flow supply of real balances.[1] This implies an increased supply of labor and a decreased demand for goods.

In terms of the equation system (11) this implies that the first two equations are not fulfilled, since the demand for goods which the firms expect, y^{De}, is now higher than the actual demand level, and the supply of labor expected by the firms, x^{Se}, is lower than the actual supply. Prices and wages are thus set on the basis of erroneous expectations. Neither is the fourth equation fulfilled. The firms now produce more than what is demanded by the households. The firms are therefore subject to a binding restriction on their sales.

For the case when the firms demand the same number of labor hours as they

---

[1] In equilibrium the flow demand for real balances is equal to the flow supply. At the same time, the flow demand for real balances is equal to the amount of increases of nominal monetary balances necessary to compensate for the higher price level expected in the next period owing to the expected rate of inflation.

would if their expectations about the demand for their products and the supply of labor by their employees were correct, the equation system describing the Keynesian equilibrium solution could be written as:

$$y^D < y^{De}$$

$$x^S > x^{Se}$$

$$W = W(y^{De}, x^{Se})$$

$$P = P(y^{De}, x^{Se})$$

$$F(x^{Se}) = y^{De}$$

$$\pi = y^{D'} - wx^{Se}$$

$$wx^{Se} + \pi + m^S - y^{D'} - m^{D'} = 0$$

$$y^{D'} = y^{D'}\left(w, 1, R, \pi + wx_0^S + m^S, \left(\frac{M}{P} + m_0^D\right)R, x^{Se}\right)$$

$$x^{S'} = x^{Se}$$

$$m^{D'} = m^{D'}\left(w, 1, R, \pi + wx_0^S + m^S, \left(\frac{M}{P} + m_0^D\right)R, x^{Se}\right) \tag{12a}$$

There is no longer equilibrium in the goods and labor markets. Nominal demand for goods is lower than the amount of goods which the firms expect to be able to sell. The nominal supply of labor is greater than the amount which the firms plan to purchase and actually purchase. The wage rate and the price level are no longer adjusted to the actual demand for goods and the actual supply of labor, but set at the levels which would maximize profits at the demand and supply levels expected by the firms. It should be noted that the fifth equation no longer gives information about the actual level of production, but instead of its planned level. Since the firms demand more labor hours than necessary for the now depressed production level there will be concealed underemployment within the firms.

The sixth equation is a definition of real profits. *Ex ante* it is a Keynesian equilibrium condition stating that effective demand for commodities should equal the national income (net of transfers used for accumulation of nominal balances):

$$wx^{Se} + \pi = y^{D'} \tag{13a}$$

Inserting this into the seventh equation of (12a), the aggregate budget equation, the equilibrium condition is that *ex ante* effective excess demand for real balances should equal zero:

$$m^S - m^{D'} = 0 \tag{14a}$$

Recalling that the flow supply of money is assumed to increase nominal balances by the same percentage as the expected rate of inflation, (14a) implies that the flow demand for real balances should be zero for the special case when the expected rate of inflation is equal to zero. But the flow demand for real balances is the same thing as household saving. Furthermore, since investments are zero, we could say that (14a) produces the *ex ante* Keynesian equilibrium condition that saving should equal investments.

Since labor income is fixed, real profits are the only variable component of national income, $dy^{D'} = d\pi$. By differentiating (13a) or (14a) with respect to a shift variable, the usual multiplier expression is obtained. The effect of e.g. increased real balances is given by:

$$m_4^{D'} dy^{D'} + (m_4^{D'} - 1) Rd \left(\frac{M}{P} \right) = 0 \quad \text{where } m_4^{D'} = MPS$$

or

$$dy^{D'} = \frac{MPC}{1 - MPC} Rd \left(\frac{M}{P} \right) \quad \text{where } y_4^{D'} = MPC \quad \text{and } m_4^{D'} + y_4^{D'} = 1 \tag{15a}$$

In the usual Keynesian analysis, employment is assumed to be instantaneously adjusted to variations in effective demand for goods. In this case, the economy is described by the following system of equations:

$$y^D < y^{De}$$
$$x^S > x^{Se}$$
$$W = W(y^{De}, x^{Se})$$
$$P = P(y^{De}, x^{Se})$$
$$F(x^{D'}) = y^{D'}$$
$$\pi = y^{D'} - wx^{S'}$$
$$wx^{S'} + \pi + m^S - y^{D'} - m^{D'} = 0$$
$$y^{D'} = y^{D'} \left(w, 1, R, \pi + wx_0^S + m^S, \left(\frac{M}{P} + m^D \right) R, x^{D'} \right)$$
$$x^{S'} = x^{D'}$$
$$m^{D'} = m^{D'} \left(w, 1, R, \pi + wx_0^S + m^S, \left(\frac{M}{P} + m_0^D \right) R, x^{D'} \right) \tag{12b}$$

The system (12b) essentially differs from (12a) only by the way in which the number of labor hours is determined. *Ceteris paribus*, the number of labor hours and labor income are lower according to (12b) than according to (12a), but profits are higher.

The sixth equation of (12b) determines the profit level, but is also a

Keynesian equilibrium condition saying that the national income should equal effective aggregate demand:

$$wx^{S'} + \pi = y^{D'} \tag{13b}$$

If instead we insert the sixth equation into the seventh, the equivalent Keynesian equilibrium condition as to flow supply and demand for real balances appears:

$$m^S - m^{D'} = 0 \tag{14b}$$

By differentiating (13b) or (14b) with respect to national income and real balances, the multiplier effect of increased real balances emerges:

$$dy^{D'} = \frac{F_1 MPC}{MPS(F_1 - w) + m_6^{D'}} Rd\left(\frac{M}{P}\right) \tag{15b}$$

(15b) will generally differ from (15a). This means that the multiplier effect differs between the case where employment is adjusted to the changed level of effective demand and the case where it is predetermined. In the special case where the marginal productivity of labor is equal to the real wage rate and the effect on household behavior is not dependent on whether an increased income is caused by profit increases or increased employment $(wm_4^{D'} = m_6^{D'})$, the values of the multipliers will coincide, however.

IV.3. *General Excess Demand*

Contrary to the Keynesian underemployment case, it is now assumed that the decisions of the imperfectly informed firms have led to price and wage levels which are too low. To simplify, we assume that the real wage level is initially set at the general equilibrium level.[1] Real balances will then be too high and the households will try to deplete them. Since the flow supply of nominal monetary balances is proportional to the stock of nominal balances, the factor or proportion being equal to the expected rate of inflation, the *ex ante* flow demand for real balances will be lower than the flow supply. The fact that the real balances are too high further means a decreased supply of labor and an increased demand for goods, cf. (2). The situation at general excess demand is described by the equation system (16):

$$y^D > y^{De}$$

$$x^S < x^{Se}$$

$$W = W(y^{De}, x^{Se})$$

$$P = P(y^{De}, x^{Se})$$

$$F(x^{S''}) = y^{S''}$$

$$\pi = y^{D''} - wx^{S''}$$

---

[1] This assumption is made throughout. It excludes the possibility of classical underemployment.

$$wx^{S''} + \pi + m^S - y^{D''} - m^{D''} = 0$$

$$y^{D''} = y^{S''}$$

$$x^{S''} = x^{S''}\left(w, 1, R, \pi + wx_0^S + m^S, \left(\frac{M}{P} + m_0^D\right)R, y^{S''}\right)$$

$$m^{D''} = m^{D''}\left(w, 1, R, \pi + wx_0^S + m^S, \left(\frac{M}{P} + m_0^D\right)R, y^{S''}\right) \tag{16}$$

The interpretation of (16) is straightforward. Note the fifth equation that states that production is constrained by the supply of labor, and the eighth equation saying that consumption is depressed to the level of production.

To get the effect on the national income of increased real balances we differentiate the fifth equation of (16) with respect to national income and real balances (note that the production level is now determined from the supply side):

$$dy^{S''} = \frac{1}{1 - \dfrac{\partial F}{\partial x^{S''}}\dfrac{\partial x^{S''}}{\partial y^{S''}} - (F' - w)\dfrac{\partial x^{S''}}{\partial \pi}}\,\frac{\partial F}{\partial x^{S''}}\,\frac{\partial x^{S''}}{\partial\left(\dfrac{M}{P}\right)}\,d\left(\frac{M}{P}\right) \tag{17}$$

The first two terms of this equation constitute the Barro-Grossman supply multiplier.

V. The Dynamics of Inflation under Keynesian Underemployment and General Excess Demand

The discussion of the preceding section concerned the quantity adjustment following a disturbance and forcing the economy out of general equilibrium. The reason why a sudden increase or decrease of initial nominal balances would not immediately bring the economy to a new general equilibrium situation, was that prices and wage rates did not instantaneously respond to the new situation. Firms set prices and wage rates so as to maximize profits, but their expectations about the appearance and location of the demand for goods and supply of labor which they are confronted by may be wrong. When expectations successively adjust (cf. equation (10)) to the new situation, the economy may, via price and wage adjustments, be brought back to a general equilibrium situation. If prices and wage rates are imperfectly flexible (but *not* inflexible), quantities instantaneously respond to variations in real balances. The demand multiplier operates under general excess supply, depressing national income and causing involuntary underemployment. Under general excess demand the supply multiplier depresses national income and causes involuntary underconsumption.

The dynamic adjustment of prices and wage rates, and the consequences for quantity adjustment, will now be studied. It should be noted, however that the rate of wage inflation will be equal to the rate of price inflation. This depends on the assumption in Section III that the real wage rate will approximately be unaffected by variations in y^{De} and x^{Se}. To simplify, it is assumed that the length of the time period tends towards zero, so that time is continuous. The equations (9) may then be rewritten so as to describe the rates of price and wage inflation:

$$g_P = g^e + \frac{\partial P}{\partial y^{De}} \dot{y}^{De} + \frac{\partial P}{\partial x^{Se}} \dot{x}^{Se} \quad \text{where } g_p = \frac{\dot{P}}{P}$$

$$g_w = g^e + \frac{\partial W}{\partial y^{De}} \dot{y}^{De} + \frac{\partial W}{\partial x^{Se}} \dot{x}^{Se} \quad \text{where } g_w = \frac{\dot{W}}{W} \tag{18}$$

where the dot indicates a time derivative. The first equation of (18) states that the actual rate of price inflation will be equal to the expected rate of price inflation plus the unexpected rate of price inflation following revisions of the expectations about goods demand and supply of labor. Falling expectations of goods demand and increasing expectations of supply of labor will cause price inflation to be lower than that expected by the firms and households. The second equation of (18) can be interpreted analogously. The expectations are adjusted via the following equations:

$$\dot{y}^{De} = \alpha(y^{D'} - y^* + y^* - y^{De}) \quad \text{for } P > P^*$$

$$\dot{y}^{De} = \alpha(y^D - y^* + y^* - y^{De}) \quad \text{for } P < P^*$$

$$\dot{x}^{Se} = \beta(x^S - x^* + x^* - x^{Se}) \quad \text{for } P > P^*$$

$$\dot{x}^{Se} = \beta(x^{S''} - x^* + x^* - x^{Se}) \quad \text{for } P < P^* \tag{19}$$

where general equilibrium values of the variables are indicated by an asterisk.

It is important to note that the actual demand under Keynesian underemployment, $y^{D'}$, is the effective demand for goods. Under general excess demand, the actual demand for goods observed by the firms, is the notional demand (which is partly unsatisfied due to the too low volume of production). Likewise, the actual supply of labor which the firms observe is equal to the notional supply under general excess supply (the notional supply of labor being partly unsatisfied by the too low demand for labor), whereas the observed supply of labor under general excess demand is equal to the effective supply of labor. The basic assumption is that the firms observe the effective supply or demand on the short side of the market and, in addition, are able to observe the wishes on the long side of the market. For example, the firms observe their own selling under general excess supply and take that as an indication of the level of demand. Under general excess demand they not only observe their own sales but, in addition, the amount of unsatisfied demand.

Noting that $y^{D'}$, y^D, x^S and $x^{S''}$ all depend on the price level, which in turn is a function of the expectations of the firms of the level of demand for goods and supply of labor (cf. (9)), (19) may be rewritten as:[1]

$$\dot{y}^{De} = \alpha \left[a_i \left(\frac{\partial P}{\partial y^{De}} (y^{De} - y^*) + \frac{\partial P}{\partial x^{Se}} (x^{Se} - x^*) \right) + y^* - y^{De} \right], \quad i = 1, 2$$

$$\dot{x}^{Se} = \beta \left[b_i \left(\frac{\partial P}{\partial y^{De}} (y^{De} - y^*) + \frac{\partial P}{\partial x^{Se}} (x^{Se} - x^*) \right) + x^* - x^{Se} \right], \quad i = 1, 2 \tag{20}$$

where[2]

$$a_1 = \frac{1}{1 - \dfrac{dy^{D'}}{\partial (M/P)}} \frac{\partial y^{D'}}{\partial (M/P)} \frac{\partial (M/P)}{\partial P} \frac{1}{P^*}, \quad P > P^*$$

$$a_2 = \frac{\partial y^D}{\partial (M/P)} \frac{\partial (M/P)}{\partial P} \frac{1}{P^*}, \quad P < P^*$$

$$b_1 = \frac{\partial x^S}{\partial (M/P)} \frac{\partial (M/P)}{\partial P} \frac{1}{P^*}, \quad P > P^*$$

$$b_2 = \frac{1}{1 - \dfrac{\partial F}{\partial x^{S'}} \dfrac{\partial x^{S'}}{\partial y^{S'}} - (F' - w) \dfrac{\partial x^{S'}}{\partial \pi}} \frac{\partial x^{S'}}{\partial (M/P)} \frac{\partial (M/P)}{\partial P} \frac{1}{P^*}, \quad P < P^* \tag{21}$$

It should be noted that effective demand under excess supply and effective supply under excess demand will be extra sensitive to variations in real balances due to the demand multiplier and the supply multiplier, respectively. It is further assumed that the two possible demand multipliers coincide, so that it is not necessary to treat the two possible cases separately. The differential equations (20) give phase-curves with the following slopes:

$$\frac{dy^{De}}{dx^{Se}} \bigg|_{\dot{y}^{De} = 0} = k_i = - \frac{\partial P / \partial x^{Se}}{(\partial P / \partial y^{De}) - (1/a_i)} > 0 \qquad \begin{matrix} i = 1 \text{ for } P > P^* \\ i = 2 \text{ for } P < P^* \end{matrix}$$

$$\frac{dy^{De}}{x^{Se}} \bigg|_{\dot{x}^{Se} = 0} = m_i = - \frac{(\partial P / \partial x^{Se}) - (1/b_i)}{\partial P / \partial y^{De}} > 0 \qquad \begin{matrix} i = 1 \text{ for } P > P^* \\ i = 2 \text{ for } P < P^* \end{matrix} \tag{22}$$

Finally the x^{Se}, y^{De}-plane should be demarcated to show which parts imply excess supply and excess demand, respectively. Starting from a general equilibrium situation, a price increase will, via the real balance effect imply general excess supply and a price decrease general excess demand. Since the price level depends on the expectations of the firms about the level of demand for goods and supply of labor, respectively, the difference

---

[1] Note for example that linear expansion around the point of general equilibrium gives:

$$y^D - y^* = - \frac{\partial y^D}{\partial (M/P)} \left(\frac{M}{P} - \left(\frac{M}{P} \right)^* \right) = \frac{\partial y^D}{\partial (M/P)} \frac{\partial (M/P)}{\partial P} \frac{(P - P^*)}{P^*}$$

$$= \frac{\partial y^D}{\partial (M/P)} \frac{\partial (M/P)}{\partial P} \frac{1}{P^*} \left[\frac{\partial P}{\partial y^{De}} (y^{De} - y^*) + \frac{\partial P}{\partial x^{Se}} (x^{Se} - x^*) \right], \quad P < P^*$$

[2] It holds unequivocally that $|a_1| > |a_2|$ and $|b_1| < |b_2|$.

between the actual price level and the general equilibrium price level can (locally) be expressed as a linear function of the difference between the expected levels and the general equilibrium levels of demand for goods, and supply of labor, respectively:

$$\frac{P - P^*}{P^*} = \frac{\partial P}{\partial y^{De}} (y^{De} - y^*) + \frac{\partial P}{\partial x^{Se}} (x^{Se} - x^*) \tag{23}$$

where $P - P^* > 0$ implies general excess supply, $P - P^* = 0$ general equilibrium, and $P - P^* < 0$ implies general excess demand. To get the locus of points in the x^{Se}, y^{De}-plane where the price level is consistent with general equilibrium we just set $P - P^*$ equal to zero in (23) and solve for y^{De}, x^{Se}. The slope of the demarcation line between the general excess supply set and the general excess demand set is given by:

$$\frac{dy^{De}}{dx^{Se}} = k_0 = -\frac{\partial P / \partial x^{Se}}{\partial P / \partial y^{De}} > 0 \tag{24}$$

Comparing the slopes of the phase curves and the line of demarcation it follows from (21), (22), and (24) that $m_1 > m_2 > k_0 > k_1 > k_2$. Geometrically, the phase curves and the line of demarcation are given in Fig. 1.

Note the important and unusual phenomenon that the phase curves are kinked as they pass the general equilibrium values of x^{Se}, y^{De}. This is due to the fact analyzed above, that multiplier effects will be switched on/switched off as we follow a phase curve and pass the intersection with the demarcation line. As usual, the arrows symbolize the forces working on x^{Se}, y^{De} in the different sectors of the diagram. These forces are determined by the equations (20).

It is obvious from the diagram that the equilibrium is stable. The trajectory in the x^{Se}, y^{De}-plane will always converge towards the equilibrium situation. Convergence will moreover be direct, without any oscillations.

It may be instructive to follow the adjustment process for some particular case. Assume that there has been a sudden fall of initial monetary balances. There will then be excess supply both in the goods and the labor markets of the individual firms. Since the expectations of the firms only gradually adjust, they will initially be fixed at the original levels, and consequently so will the price and the wage level. Since (due to the fall of initial nominal balances) the general equilibrium price level is now lower than the original price leve, the firms think that the demand for their goods is greater and that the supply of labor by their employees is smaller than is actually the case. The original disturbance will thus shift x^{Se}, y^{De} upwards and to the left; cf. point 1 in Fig. 1.[1] At the same time, there will be a downward shift of

---

[1] The expected demand for goods is constant with respect to the original equilibrium price level but has increased in terms of the new lower general equilibrium price level. The same holds, *mutatis mutandis*, for the expectations of the firms about the supply of labor of their employees.

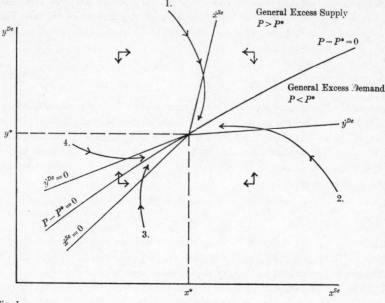

Fig. 1.

purchases from y^* to $y^{D'}$ via the (demand) multiplier. This shift is not shown in the figure. Since the effective demand for goods is now lower than the demand expected by the firms and since the nominal supply of labor is higher than expected, the firms will successively revise their goods demand expectations downwards and their labor supply expectations upwards. This implies that they will decrease their prices in comparison to the trend set by the expected rate of inflation. Since price increases equal to the expected rate of inflation would suffice to balance the rate of increase of nominal balances, real balances will increase. As long as the actual rate of inflation is lower than the expected rate, real balances increase, and the effective demand for goods increases, whereas the supply of labor decreases. The gaps between the actual and expected demand for goods and supply of labor, respectively, will fall continuously and this implies that the amount of unexpected price deflation will fall as the new general equilibrium is approached.

If the expected rate of price inflation is allowed to change according to the gap between the actual and the expected rate of inflation, one would expect inflationary expectations to continually decrease during a phase of general excess supply.

Since the actual rate of inflation is then lower than the expected rate, inflationary expectations will continually be revised downwards during the transition towards general equilibrium. It is then probable that the expected rate of inflation will be lower than the rate of expansion of nominal balances when general equilibrium is attained. If this is the case, the equilibrium will be overshot, leading to general excess demand. The introduction of adaptive expectations of inflation would thus imply oscillations.

References

Arrow, K. J.: Toward a theory of price adjustment. In Moses Abramovitz (ed.), *The allocation of economic resources.* Stanford University Press, Stanford, 1959.

Barro, R. J. & Grossman, H. I.: A general disequilibrium model of income and employment. *American Economic Review*, March 1971.

Clower, R.: The Keynesian counterrevolution: A theoretical appraisal. In F. H. Hahn and F. P. R. Brechling (eds.), *The theory of interest rates.* Macmillan, London, 1965.

Löfgren, K.-G.; Inflation, unemployment and expectations a neo-Keynesian version. Stencil, Umeå, 1975.

Patinkin, D.: *Money, interest, and prices.* Harper & Row, New York, 1965.

Phelps, E. S. (ed.): *Microeconomic foundations of employment and inflation theory.* W. W. Norton & Co, New York, 1970.

Samuelson, P. A.: *Foundations of economic analysis.* Harvard University Press, Cambridge, 1947.

Siven, C.-H.: *A study in the theory of inflation and unemployment.* Stockholm, 1975.

Siven, C.-H.: *Stochastic structural disequilibria and the interaction between multiplier and inflation processes.* Working paper, Stockholm, 1976.

Tobin, J. & Houthakker, H. S.: The effects of rationing on demand elasticities. *Review of Economic Studies*, 1950–51.

THE STABILITY OF A DISEQUILIBRIUM IS-LM MODEL*

Hal R. Varian

University of Michigan, Ann Arbor, Michigan, USA

Abstract

A disequilibrium version of the standard IS-LM model is constructed and used to analyze the stability of the model. The main feature of the disequilibrium behavior turns out to be a spillover from the money market to the output market; if there is an excess demand for loanable funds (or an excess supply of bonds) firms will be unable to finance all of their desired investment, and aggregate demand will therefore be smaller than would otherwise be the case. This spillover has certain implications for the dynamic behavior of the model.

I. Introduction

The purpose of this paper is to analyze the stability of an IS-LM type macro-economic model. If we are to analyze what happens when such a system is perturbed from equilibrium, we need to have a consistent story about what happens in such a model when we are out of equilibrium. Thus we need first to construct a disequilibrium version of the IS-LM model.

The recent literature on disequilibrium behavior has emphasized the importance of "spillovers". When one market fails to clear, rational economic agents may revise the demands and supplies that they present to other markets. These spillover effects have been ignored in the standard IS-LM stability analysis. We shall see that this has tended to "overstate" the stability of the IS-LM model.

Other disequilibrium models in the literature include: Barro & Grossman (1971), Benassy (1973), Korliras (1975), Solow & Stiglitz (1968), and Varian (1977). Not surprisingly, the model described here is most closely related to this last work.

---

* A previous version of this paper was entitled "A Disequilibrium Macroeconomic Model". This work was supported in part by Bell Telephone Laboratories, Murray Hill, New Jersey and in part by the National Science Foundation.

In my view the classical belief that the economy is usually at or near some sort of "equilibrium" is in some sense correct. But *which* equilibrium the economy is at depends on the stability properties of the equilibria. Since otherwise desirable equilibria may be unstable, an analysis of the factors affecting instability is rather important. Such an analysis can only be done when one has a model of disequilibrium behavior. The model presented here is hopefully a step towards describing such behavior.

II. The Disequilibrium Model

The goal is to describe a very simple disequilibrium model that is compatible with the equilibrium behavior of the simple IS-LM model. To that end we adopt the usual assumptions of the IS-LM model. There are two flow goods, labor (N) and a homogeneous output good (Y) that can be either consumed or invested. There are no inventories. The capital stock is taken to be fixed so that output depends on labor through a neoclassical production function of the standard sort, $f(N)$. The nominal stock of money (M) is taken to be given. The time period under consideration is short enough so that the firms' stock of capital is not significantly affected by the flow of investment and the consumers' stock of wealth is not significantly affected by the flow of savings.

The *state* of the economy is a four-vector $s = (P, W, r, y)$ where P is the nominal price of output, W is the nominal wage rate, r is the interest rate, and y represents the agents' expectations about the level of demand. This last variable is of crucial importance and deserves further discussion.

In classical general equilibrium models firm behavior depends only on a vector of relative prices. This may be reasonable in equilibrium, but in a disequilibrium situation, markets will not all clear and economic agents will be unable to complete their desired transactions. Rational economic agents will presumably take this possibility into account and attempt to forecast the level of transactions; this is the role played by the expectation y. In order to make rational decisions firms need to forecast both the current and the future demand for output; the first in order to determine how much current output to produce, and the second to determine how much investment to undertake in order to produce future output. In a world with complete, continually equilibrated futures markets the investment decision depends only on a vector of futures prices. In a world with no futures markets, firms must guess at the level of future demand. A good indicator of this future demand is presumably current demand; hence investment decisions will depend on firms' expectations about current demand, and the variable y will be a relevant state variable.

The outcome of certain market activities may affect subsequent behavior. For this reason we will describe the functioning of the model in several stages.

Stage 1. *The determination of intended actions*

A. *The firms.* First the firms must determine their demand for labor. In a purely competitive, continually equilibrated world the demand for labor would depend only on the real wage. In this model firms are aware of the possibility of disequilibrium and base their demand for labor on the real wage and their expectations concerning the final demand for output. Hence we write the aggregate demand for labor as $N_d(W/P, y)$.

More precisely, each firm maximizes its profits subject to the constraint that it produces no more than its market share of the expected demand. Thus the unconstrained, aggregate demand for labor will be given by $N_d(W/P, \infty)$ and the constrained demand for labor would be given by $N_d(W/P, y) = \min(f^{-1}(y), N_d(W/P, \infty))$.

Secondly, the firms determine their demand for capital—that is, their demand for output to be used for investment. In general this demand will depend on W/P, r and y, so we will write it as $ID(s)$. This is interpreted as the demand for real output for investment purposes as a function of the state of the economy.

We assume that firms must finance their investment by borrowing—that is by issuing new bonds. Hence a demand for investment will give rise to a supply of new bonds. We assume bonds are perpetuities issued in face amounts of one dollar and sell at a price $P_B = 1/r$. Let B be the number of new bonds issued. Then B/r will be the amount of money realized by the sale of the bonds, and B/rP will be the amount of output that can be purchased with this money. We will measure the supply of new bonds in terms of real output, so that $B_s(s) \equiv B/rP \equiv ID(s)$.

B. *The consumers.* At this stage the consumers first determine a planned supply of labor which we denote by $N_s(W/P)$. Secondly, the consumers determine how they wish to divide their portfolio between money and bonds. The outcome of this decision about *stocks* of assets will give rise to a decision about *flows*—namely, about how many bonds to acquire or divest. This decision about changes in portfolio balance will generate a demand for the *new* bonds issued by the firms. We will assume that the excess demand for *new* bonds has the same sign as the excess demand for *all* bonds. We write this demand for new bonds as $B_d(r, y)$. As in the usual model, the real demand for bonds is taken to depend on the interest rate and the expected level of real income. The demand for new bonds is measured in terms of real output, just as we measured the supply of new bonds.

Stage 2. *The determinasion of effective actions*

We have now determined the intentions of the economic agents at an arbitrary state of the economy. We now exmine how these intended demands and supplies interact.

A. *The firms.* If the demand for newly issued bonds does not equal the supply of newly issued bonds, firms will not be able to finance their desired amount of investment. The actual amount of investment financed—the effective investment demand—will be given by:

$$I_d(s) = \min\left(ID(s),\ B_d(r, y)\right)$$

Similarly if the demand for labor is not equal to the supply of labor the actual amount of labor sold will be equal to:

$$N(s) = \min\left(N_s(W/P),\ N_d(W/P, y)\right)$$

The income of consumers will be given by the sum of labor income plus profit income. Profit income is taken to include interest payments on bonds. Hence consumers' income will be given by:

$$PY(s) = WN(s) + Pf(N(s)) - WN(s)$$
$$= Pf(N(s))$$

Hence national income, $Y(s)$, equals national product, $f(N(s))$, as an accounting identity, as one would expect.

B. *The Consumers.* Once real income $Y(s)$ is determined, consumers can determine their real demand for output for consumption. We write this as $C_d(Y(s))$.

Stage 3. *The market adjustments*

If the expectations about the demand for output are not equal to the actual demand for output we will assume that firms adjust their expectations by some sign preserving function of the gap:

$$\dot{y} = G_0[C_d(f(N(W/P, y)) + I_d(W/P, r, y) - y]$$

If the demand for output is not equal to the supply of output, the price level also adjusts:

$$\dot{P} = G_1[C_d(f(N(W/P, y)) + I_d(W/P, r, y) - f(N(W/P, y))]$$

If the demand for new bonds is not equal to the supply of new bonds the interest rate adjusts:

$$\dot{r} = G_2[B_s(W/P, r, y) - B_d(r, y)]$$

Finally if the demand for labor is not equal to the supply of labor the wage rate adjusts. This adjustment is often felt to be rather slow:

$$\dot{W} = G_3[N_d(W/P, y) - N_s(W/P)]$$

We now have an adjustment equation for each state variable. We can begin to analyze the stability of the model.

III. Justification of the Model

There are several features of the model presented in the last section that need some further discussion.

1. *The role of expectations.* The classical Keynesian model can be posed purely in terms of the state variables W, P, and r. The real wage should determine labor demand and employment. This in turn determines real output. Investment demand may be taken to depend on the interest rate.

If we set up the model in this way, we would need only three state adjustment equations, and the analysis would proceed by examining the movements of W, P and r; the level of output would not be a separate state variable.

But the usual stability analysis of an IS-LM model does use national income as a state variable. If we are to make sense of this approach in a disequilibrium setting it seems that we should interpret "national income" as "expected aggregate demand".

2. *Asset flows.* The equilibrium in the asset market is characterized by the *flow demand for bonds* being in equilibrium. The usual Keynesian model characterizes equilibrium by the *stock demand for money* being in equilibrium. In this model we are interpreting the interest rate as the reciprocal of the price of bonds. Hence the movements of the interest rate should depend on the demands and supplies of bonds that are communicated to the market, namely the current flow demands.

We have also taken the movements of the interest rate to depend on the excess demand for *new* bonds. If new and old bonds are perfect substitutes, it seems that there will be excess demands on the *bond* market if and only if there is excess demand in the *new bond* market. If new and old bonds are not perfect substitutes, the price of new bonds may differ from the price of old bonds. But it is the price of new bonds that is relevant to the firms' investment decision, so the adjustment process we have proposed still makes sense.

For a comprehensive discussion of asset equilibrium in more elaborate Keynesian models see Foley (1975), Buiter & Woglam (1977) and Foley (1977).

3. *The widow's cruse.* In order to determine consumer demand we need to know what profit payments are. But we cannot know what *actual* profits are until we know what consumer demand is. One solution to this problem is to base current profit payments on last period's profits. We have taken another solution: this period's profit payments are based on firms' expected profits. This seems the most satisfactory solution for a continuous time model.

4. *Loanable funds.* The whole model can be described in terms of "loanable funds" rather than "new issues of bonds". The interpretation is that investment is financed by bank loans and the LL curve is the locus of points where the demand for loans equals the supply of loans. If there is disequilibrium in the loan market—credit rationing—desired investment demand will differ

from financed investment demand, and there will be a spillover to the output market.

In many ways this interpretation is more realistic since credit rationing of bank loans seems likely to persist for a longer time than a situation with an excess supply of new bonds. That is, the institutional restrictions on bank interest rates seem likely to make them more sticky than the prices of newly issued bonds.

IV. The Dynamic IS-LM Model

We will assume that the nominal price level and nominal wage are fixed in the short run and examine the movements of r and y.

For fixed W/P we can determine the supply of labor $N_s(W/P)$ and hence the *full employment* output $y_w = f(N_s(W/P))$. Similarly we can determine the unconstrained profit maximizing demand for labor $N_d(W/P, \infty)$ and hence the level of *full capacity* output $y_P = f(N_d(W/P, \infty))$.

If y is less than y_P, firms' expectations will actually constrain their profit maximization process and actual output will just be equal to expected demand. Hence consumers' real income will just be equal to the expected demand:

$$Y = f(N(W/P, y)) = y$$

When y is less than y_P and y_w we can write the model as:

$$\dot{y} = G_0[C_d(y) + I_d(y, r) - y]$$
$$\dot{r} = G_2[ID(y, r) - B_d(y, r)]$$

Here we have omitted the variables that are constrained to be fixed. The main difference from the standard IS-LM model seems to be the distinction between the *intended* demand for investment $ID(y, r)$ and the *effective* demand for investment. The distinction between these two investment functions arises from the spillover from the money market to the output market: if firms are unable to finance all of their intended investment due to a disequilibrium in the money market, the demand for output will be affected.

The set of points where $\dot{r} = 0$ will be called the LL curve. It is analogous to the usual LM curve since it represents those combinations of r and y that equilibrate the bond market. To find the slope of this curve, we write it as an implicit function $r_L(y)$ that must satisfy the identity:

$$ID(y, r_L(y)) - B_d(y, r_L(y)) \equiv 0$$

Differentiating, we find:

$$\frac{\partial ID(y, r)}{\partial y} + \frac{\partial ID(y, r)}{\partial r} \frac{dr_L(y)}{dy} - \frac{\partial B_d(y, r)}{\partial y} - \frac{\partial B_d(y, r)}{\partial r} \frac{dr_L(y)}{dy} = 0$$

$$\frac{dr_L(y)}{dy} = \frac{\overset{(-)}{(\partial B_d(y, r)/\partial y)} - \overset{(+)}{(\partial ID(y, r)/\partial y)}}{\underset{(-)}{(\partial ID(y, r)/\partial r)} - \underset{(+)}{(\partial B_d(y, r)/\partial r)}}$$

In the usual IS-LM model we assume that $\partial B_d(y, r)/\partial y$ is negative due to the transactions demand for money. The other signs are standard. We see that the LL curve will have a positive slope.

The set of points where $\dot{y} = 0$ will be called the YY curve. It is analogous to the usual IS curve since it represents those combinations of y and r that equilibrate the output market. To find the slope of this curve we let $r_Y(y)$ be the implicit function that satisfies the identity:

$$C_d(y) + I_d(y, r_Y(y)) - y \equiv 0$$

$$\frac{dC_d(y)}{dy} + \frac{\partial I_d(y, r)}{\partial y} + \frac{\partial I_d(y, r)}{\partial r} \frac{dr_Y(y)}{dy} - 1 = 0$$

$$\frac{dr_Y(y)}{dy} = \frac{1 - (dC_d(y)/dy) - (\partial I_d(y, r)/\partial y)}{\partial I_d(y, r)/\partial r}$$

The slope of the YY curve depends on whether we are above or below the LL curve. For if we are above the LL curve, $I_d(y, r)$ will equal $ID(y, r)$ and $\partial I_d(y, r)/\partial y$ will be positive and $\partial I_d(y, r)/\partial r$ will be negative; but when we are below the LL curve, investment demand will be constrained by the demand for bonds and $I_d(y, r)$ will equal $B_d(y, r)$. Hence $\partial I_d(y, r)/\partial y$ will be negative since $\partial B_d(y, r)/\partial y$ is negative, and the sign of $\partial I_d(y, r)/\partial r$ will be positive since the sign of $\partial B_d(y, r)/\partial r$ is presumably positive. The slope of the Y_1Y curve will be given by:

$$\frac{dr_Y(y)}{dy} = \begin{cases} \left[1 - \underset{(+)}{\frac{dC_d(y)}{dy}} - \underset{(+)}{\frac{\partial ID(y, r)}{\partial y}} \right] \Big/ \underset{(-)}{\frac{\partial ID(y, r)}{\partial r}} & \text{if } (y, r) \text{ is above } LL \\[3mm] \left[1 - \underset{(+)}{\frac{dC_d(y)}{dy}} - \underset{(-)}{\frac{\partial B_d(y, r)}{\partial y}} \right] \Big/ \underset{(+)}{\frac{\partial B_d(y, r)}{\partial r}} & \text{if } (y, r) \text{ is below } LL \end{cases}$$

Below the LL curve, the slope of the YY curve is certainly positive, at least as long as the marginal propensity to consume is less than one. Above the LL curve, the slope of the YY curve depends on the usual thing, namely

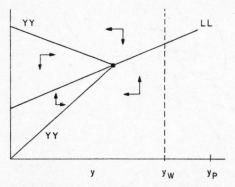

Fig. 1. Disequilibrium dynamics – unique equilibrium.

whether the marginal propensity to consume plus the marginal propensity to invest is greater or less than one.

Let us suppose that $MPC + MPI < 1$ for all the states above the LL curve. Then the shapes of the curves will be as in Fig. 1. The equilibrium values of r and y should be the same as the equilibrium values in the standard IS-LM model; only the dynamics will be different.

In Fig. 1 I have depicted the movements of the state variables in the various regimes. It is not hard to see that the unique equilibrium will be stable. In this case, the spillover effects have changed the quantitative effects of the dynamics, but have not changed the qualitative effects.

V. Multiple Equilibria

Let us now relax the assumption that the MPC plus MPI is everywhere less than one. When we allow the IS curve to have regions of positive slope

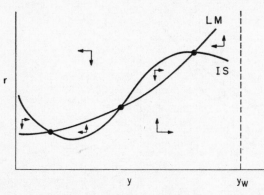

Fig. 2. IS-LM dynamics – multiple equilibria.

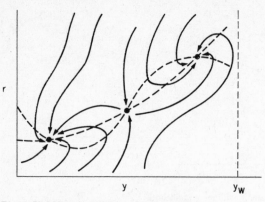

Fig. 3. IS-LM trajectories – multiple equilibria.

it is easy to get multiple equilibria. I have illustrated an example of such multiple equilibria in Fig. 2. Some possible trajectories associated with such an equilibrium configuration are given in Fig. 3. Of course the dynamic pictures in Figs. 2 and 3 are the standard IS-LM dynamics which ignores the spillovers.

The YY and LL curves represent the "true" disequilibrium dynamic structure of an IS-LM model. Fig. 4 shows what these curves would look like in a multiple equilibrium case. The locations of the equilibria in Fig. 4 are exactly the same as the locations of the equilibria in Fig. 2. The portions of the YY curve that are above the LL curve coincide exactly with the analagous portions of the IS curve. Only below the LL curve is the shape of the YY curve different. Fig. 5 gives some possible trajectories associated with the dynamics illustrated in Fig. 4.

Some inspection of Figs. 4 and 5 suggests that the disequilibrium dynamics

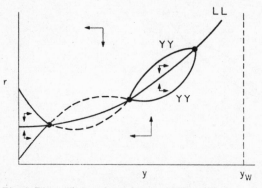

Fig. 4. Disequilibrium dynamics – multiple equilibria.

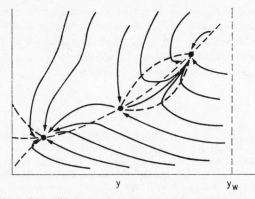

Fig. 5. Disequilibrium trajectories – multiple equilibria.

is "more unstable" than the standard, no spillover dynamics in the sense that $\dot{y}$ is negative over a larger region of the state space. When we take into account the spillover effect, national income tends to fall more often than the standard dynamics might suggest.

This is in fact a general proposition. National income falls when savings exceeds investment. In the disequilibrium model savings can exceed investment for two reasons: either (1) consumers want to save more than firms want to invest; or (2) firms *want* to invest more than consumers want to save but they are unable to finance their desired investment. The standard dynamics takes account only of reason (1), while the disequilibrium dynamics takes account of both reasons.

Consider an arbitrary state of the economy where desired savings exceeds desired investment. Since effective investment is bounded above by desired investment, desired savings also exceeds effective investment. Hence national income will fall in both the standard and the disequilibrium dynamic models. This shows that the region of downward instability is at least as large in the disequilibrium model as in the standard model. If the financial spillover is sufficiently binding, the region of downward instability will be strictly larger. In this sense, the standard dynamics understates the instability of the IS-LM model.

VI. Summary

We have constructed a simple disequilibrium version of the standard IS-LM model and used it to analyze the stability of the macroeconomic equilibria. The main distinction from the standard stability analysis has been the recognition that disequilibrium in the bond market may "spill over" into the output market: if firms cannot finance all of their intended investment, actual investment demand will be less than desired investment demand.

124   *H. R. Varian*

If there is a unique equilibrium and the standard macrostability condition is globally satisfied, the unique equilibrium will be stable. If there are multiple equilibria some will be stable and some will be unstable; but, the region of the state space where aggregate demand declines will be larger when the disequilibrium spillover is taken into account than when it is not.

References

Barro, R. & Grossman, H.: A general disequilibrium model of income and employment. *American Economic Review 61*, 82–93, 1971.

Benassy, J. P.: *Disequilibrium theory*, Ph.D. Dissertation, University of California at Berkeley, 1973.

Buiter, W. & Woglam, G.: On two specifications of asset equilibrium in macroeconomic models. *Journal of Political Economy 85*, 395–400, 1977.

Foley, D.: On two specifications of asset equilibrium in macroeconomic models. *Journal of Political Economy 83*, 303–324, 1975.

Foley, D.: Reply to Buiter and Woglam, *Journal of Political Economy 85*, 401–402, 1977.

Korliras, P.: A disequilibrium macro model. *The Quarterly Journal of Economics*, pp. 56–80, 1975.

Solow, R. & Stiglitz, J.: Output employment and wages in the short run. *The Quarterly Journal of Economics*, pp. 537–560, 1968.

Varian, H.: Non-Walrasian equilibria. *Econometrica 45*, 573–590, 1977.